GLC
PREFERRED
DWELLING
PLANS
Second Edition

GLC
PREFERRED DWELLING PLANS

Second Edition

The Architectural Press Ltd: London

First published in Great Britain by
The Architectural Press Ltd : London 1977

Reprinted 1978

ISBN 0 85139 246 6

Department of Architecture and Civic Design of the
Greater London Council

Second Edition 1981

Printed in Great Britain by
Mackays of Chatham, Limited

Contents

Introduction
to the
Second Edition

This is a completely revised and updated edition of the Preferred Dwelling Plans, first published in book form at the beginning of 1977. Almost all the drawings have been amended to take account of feedback through continued use and experience and the opportunity has been taken to add two additional plans. These are PDP 6099, illustrating a narrow frontage dual aspect house accommodating 6 persons on 3 storeys and PDP 4201, a wider frontage two-storey house for 5 persons.

As before, these plans, and any further examples that may be added to them in future years, will be subjected to a continuous and regular process of monitoring and feedback in order to ensure that account is taken of any changes in standards or requirements. Drawings will be amended and altered wherever it is found that such changes are essential. Any enquiries relating to the contents of this book or further information about the Preferred Dwelling Plans can be obtained from:

The Information Officer
Department of Architecture and Civic Design
Greater London Council
County Hall
London, SE1

PDPs: background and objectives

The GLC Architects Department's current housing programme is being concentrated on the Docklands of East London, infill sites within the Covent Garden Action Area, and Thamesmead. The success of our efforts to meet the targets set depends greatly on the sites available, and most of the sites now coming forward for local authority housing are much smaller than the 300–500 dwelling sites that were once the norm. In order to offset the reduced productivity inherent in the development of these small sites it is vitally important to attempt to evolve a more rationalised approach.

With this in mind the range of type plans known as Preferred Dwelling Plans (PDPs) has been developed by the Department's Housing Branch. This in itself is not an innovation, as the Department has been using type plans for many years. But what is new is that this range, which has reduced the previous unwieldy number of 120 types to a total of 38, has been geared to allow a great variety of layouts on a majority of sites.

Simplification of the accommodation mixes required for site development has provided a convenient opportunity for streamlining the plan range, and the main characteristics of most housing schemes can be predicted. In the foreseeable future, housing will be limited to a maximum height of three storeys, with densities restricted to 250 ppha and below. Dwellings will be divided into two main categories: houses with gardens for families and two person flats. Directives on garaging facilities have been brought into line with recent DoE recommendations, which called for 'a reduction in the provision for cars in local authority housing'. The days of the integral garage seem to be over, indeed, in the present financial climate garages will no longer be provided at all. Instead, provision for the car will be made in the form of open hard-standings, not all of which will be built at the time that schemes are completed.

The enormous variations frequently encountered in site conditions have also been taken into consideration. The basic range of PDPs consists of house and flat plans which can be used either together or separately. The range also includes a number of standard and special corner solutions which should provide the mixture of terraces, blocks, corners and angled arrangements which contribute to the environmental quality of housing layouts.

Standardisation

The essential difference between PDPs and all previous GLC attempts at rationalising the design of dwelling types is that with PDPs, the inside of the dwelling has been fully detailed for repetitive use. The interior of each dwelling has been totally standardised and documented, from above the floor slab (inclusive of floor tiles) to the underside of the top floor ceiling board, and from side to side within the plaster or plasterboard finish of external walls and party walls. The internal elements of the dwellings have been subjected to the same level of rationalisation as the plans themselves. In all cases off-the-peg components, including straight staircases, repetitive kitchen and bathroom layouts and uniform partitions will be used.

The level of standardisation implicit in the PDP operation will not reduce the effectiveness of the arthitect's role in any way. The plan range will merely reduce wasteful duplication of design work. In layouts which use PDPs, not only will preliminary design stages be shortened but in addition, standard documentation of the dwelling types, consisting of fully prepared packages of working drawings and bills of quantities will cut the amount of repetition at the contract preparation stage.

These economies will allow the designer to spend more time on the architectural treatment of the exterior of the dwellings. An attempt has been made to standardize the external envelope by use of the *GLC Good Practice Details*, but the elevational treatment including fenestration, choice of materials and roof details, may have to be specially designed in accordance with particular site conditions and planning requirements. The design of the overall housing layout will continue to offer similar scope for original thinking, and the use of PDPs will allow more time to be spent on the actual layout development. This is an important advantage ; with the trend towards lower densities the design of the spaces between buildings has become crucial.

Standards

Standards of space, equipment and plan arrangement used in the PDP range conform with mandatory requirements, as specified in DoE circulars 21/70 and 82/69, but in cases where such standards are not mandatory, modifications have been made with a view to reducing costs, minimising production difficulties and simplifying construction arrangements. The GLC Policy Standards differ in a number of respects from DoE recommendations. GLC standards specify a minimum width of 3.2 m for living rooms. A minimum area of 8.4 m² should be provided for all members of the family to eat in a separate dining room. Double bedrooms should have a minimum width of 2.6 m, while single bedrooms should measure a minimum of 1.8 m. All six person dwellings should have four bedrooms. Internal storage space should be planned for, although not constructed.

Where heating installations are concerned, GLC standards exceed those set out in DoE Circular 27/70. GLC heating standards specify a temperature of 21°C in living rooms, and 18°C elsewhere, including bedrooms and bathrooms. Old people's dwellings should be heated throughout to the mandatory 21°C standard. Heating installations for houses should comprise an individual gas-fired boiler and radiators. For blocks of flats containing old people's accommodation a central boiler house under the landlord's control should be provided.

PDPs:
general scope

The PDP range at present consists of a total of 38 plans, and includes 26 houses and 12 flats. This revised edition comprises 22 examples including the 20 plans approved by Committee.

Houses
The selection of house plans caters for three, four, five and six persons and has been designed to take care of a number of different density requirements, ranging from approximately 250 ppha at the top of the the density scale to 120 ppha at the lower end.

At relatively high densities of 250 ppha, narrow frontage 3.600 m and medium frontage 4.800 m houses provide the most economic use of land, while at lower densities of about 180 ppha, it is possible to use a slightly wider 5.400 m frontage house type. In the case of the 3.600 m and 4.800 m types, all the dwellings are dual-aspect and can be planned in terraces with north and south entry. The 5.400 m frontage dwellings on the other hand, can be planned either with dual-aspect or with controlled-aspect. In the latter case, no habitable rooms need face each other and this gives increased flexibility in layout design. On difficult sites where there are problems of noise and aspect, single-aspect types with wide frontages of 6.600 m and over may be used, where all habitable rooms are confined to one side of the dwelling.

The PDP range also includes several end of terrace houses with side-entry. These maintain the same depth as some of the other plans, and can give elevational variation to the gable end of the dwelling. A number of obtuse-angled plans have been developed for the wider frontage houses and three-storey flats, although it is anticipated that the use of these corner types will be limited.

Flats
The range of flats is restricted to two person plans, divided into two and three-storey types. Each group provides for north and south entry. In both ranges the plans can be 'mirrored' to form semi-detached or terraced solutions.

To provide maximum flexibility of elevational design, entry arrangements to the two-storey flats can either be open or partially or fully enclosed, without affecting the internal planning of the dwellings. The three-storey range has a communal stair in every case. Where more than two flats per floor are provided, the depth becomes too great for terraced solutions and the flats can be planned as individual blocks.

The plans are designed with a view to minimising the problems of security, day-to-day cleaning and refuse disposal. The location of dustbins, either singly or in groups, in relation to entrances, can be varied to suit particular schemes.

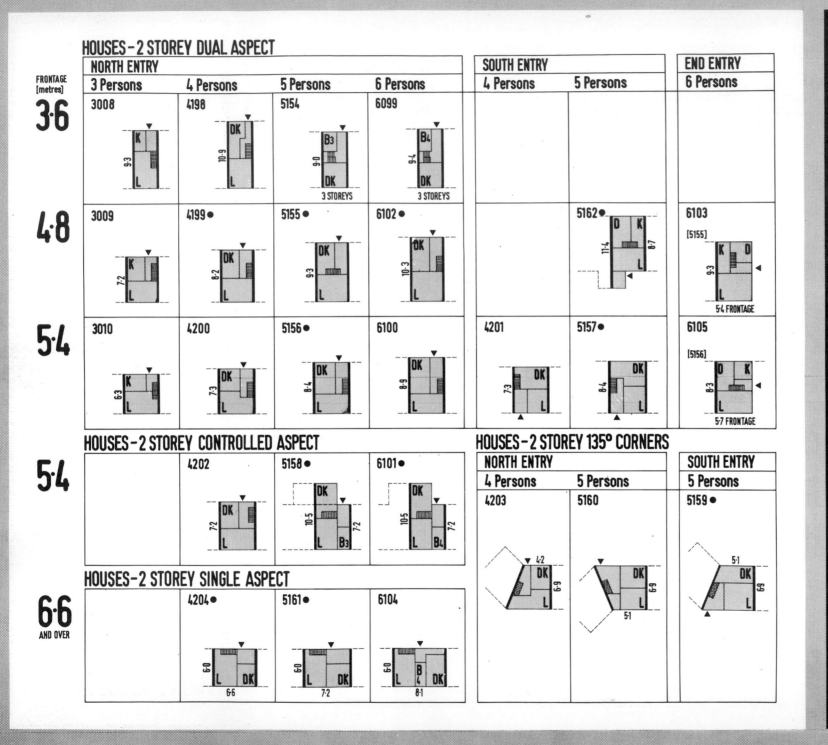

HOUSES – 2 STOREY DUAL ASPECT

FRONTAGE [metres]	NORTH ENTRY				SOUTH ENTRY		END ENTRY
	3 Persons	4 Persons	5 Persons	6 Persons	4 Persons	5 Persons	6 Persons
3·6	3008	4198	5154	6099			
			3 STOREYS	3 STOREYS			
4·8	3009	4199 ●	5155 ●	6102 ●		5162 ●	6103 [5155] 5·4 FRONTAGE
5·4	3010	4200	5156 ●	6100	4201	5157 ●	6105 [5156] 5·7 FRONTAGE

HOUSES – 2 STOREY CONTROLLED ASPECT

FRONTAGE		4 Persons	5 Persons	6 Persons
5·4		4202	5158 ●	6101 ●

HOUSES – 2 STOREY 135° CORNERS

	NORTH ENTRY		SOUTH ENTRY
	4 Persons	5 Persons	5 Persons
	4203	5160	5159 ●

HOUSES – 2 STOREY SINGLE ASPECT

FRONTAGE		4 Persons	5 Persons	6 Persons
6·6 AND OVER		4204 ●	5161 ●	6104

FLATS – 2 STOREY INDIVIDUAL STAIR APPROACH

ENCLOSED STAIR			EXT. 1/2 STAIR
NORTH ENTRY	**SOUTH ENTRY**	**SIDE ENTRY**	**NORTH ENTRY**
2210 ●	2207 ●	2225 ●	2206

TERRACE

90° EXT. NORTH ENTRY	90° EXT. SOUTH ENTRY	90° INT. NORTH ENTRY
2209 ●	2224 ●	2208 ●

CORNER

FLATS – 3 STOREY COMMUNAL STAIR APPROACH

NORTH ENTRY	SOUTH ENTRY
6 Flats	6 Flats
2211 ●	2212 ●

TERRACE

135° EXT. NORTH ENTRY	135° INT. NORTH ENTRY	135° EXT. SOUTH ENTRY
2220	2218 ●	2219

CORNER

Scale

0   10   20

PDP layout implications

Dual aspect houses

3·600 m frontage

The narrowest frontage within the PDP range is the 3.600 m house type. This type is best suited for densities of about 250 ppha. The three-storey versions are also suitable for new developments which may have to extend an existing street frontage.

The layout example illustrates the use of two-storey four person houses and three-storey five and six person houses on a rectangular site. The site is surrounded on three sides by residential roads, with no problems of access or refuse collection. The three-storey houses are planned with back-to-back gardens, spaced at a minimum distance of 21.000 m. In cases where one side of a dwelling faces a gable wall, this distance may be reduced to 12.000 m, as it is beween the two-storey four person houses and the gable end of the terrace of three-storey five person houses. The six person house is planned with the living room on the first floor.

No special single-aspect or corner plans have been developed for the narrow frontage range, as the cross-wall widths are an inhibiting factor.

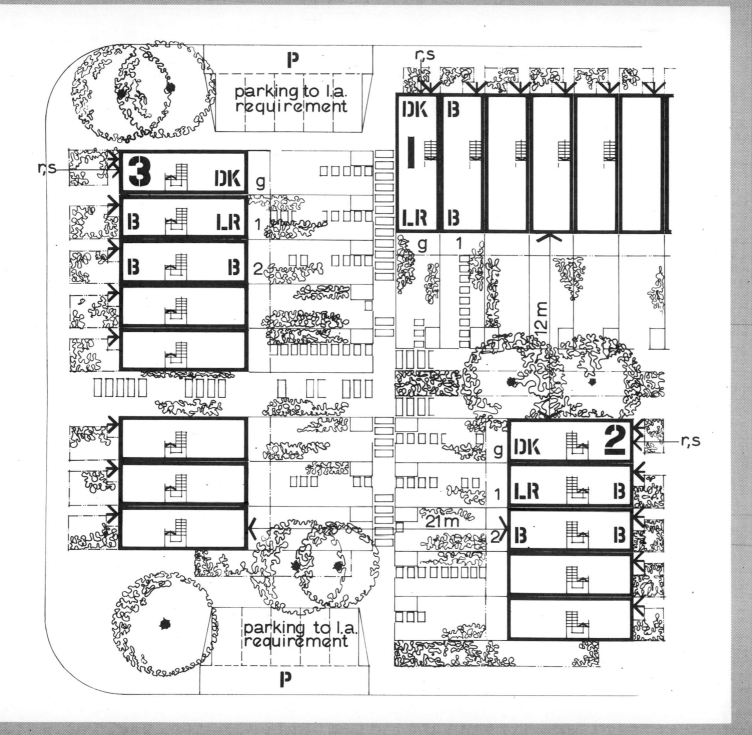

P

parking to l.a.
requirement

r,s

3 | DK | g
B | LR | 1
B | B | 2

r,s

DK | B
| |
LR | B
g | 1

12 m

21 m

DK | **2** | r,s
LR | B
B | B | 2
g
1

parking to l.a.
requirement

P

Layout implications
Dual aspect houses
3.600 m frontage

1

4 person 2 storey house
north/east/west entry
PDP 4198

2

5 person 3 storey house
north/east/west entry
PDP 5154

3

6 person 3 storey house
north/east/west entry
PDP 6099

rs

refuse collection
service entry point

Scale

0   5   10

PDP 6099

Dual aspect house

3·600 m frontage

This three-storey six person house can be planned in terraces with front door entry from north, east or west. The front door may be recessed to form a covered porch with a dustbin store if required.

The ground floor entrance hall serves the dining-kitchen and the fourth bedroom, which can also be used as study if required. The staircase is centrally situated, and there is also a ground floor WC, and a broom cupboard accessible from the hall. There is a separate store as well as a ventilated food cupboard in the dining-kitchen. The central heating boiler is positioned in the dining-kitchen.

The first floor contains the living room to the rear of the house, and the principal bedroom in the front. There is provision for storage on the landing.

The second floor contains the second and third bedrooms and the combined bathroom and WC. The double bedroom at the rear is large enough to include general storage units. The linen cupboard with hot water cylinder is positioned next to the landing.

When planning the layout, the proximity of the public footpath to the front porch and bedroom window will be subject to the positioning of the dustbin store. The length of the back garden will be determined by the privacy distance required when dual-aspect dwellings back on to each other.

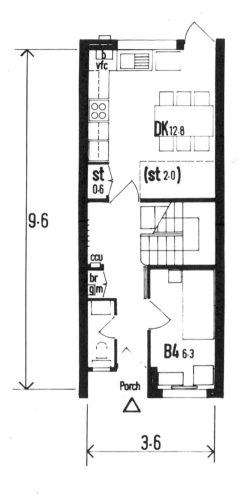

GROUND FLOOR

b
vfc

DK 12·8

st 0·6

(st 2·0)

ccu
br g/m

B4 6·3

Porch

9·6

3·6

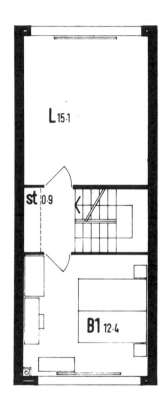

FIRST FLOOR

L 15·1

st 0·9

B1 12·4

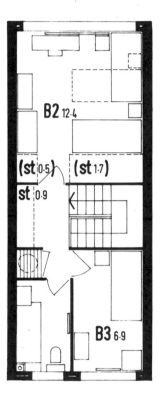

SECOND FLOOR

B2 12·4

(st 0·5)   (st 1·7)

st 0·9

B3 6·9

PDP 6099
Dual aspect
3 storey house
3·600 m frontage

6 person north entry type

Space (m²)		Mandatory	± %
Net	97·0	98·0	+1·0
Storage	5·6	4·5	

Scale

0   1   2   3   4

PDP
layout implications

Dual aspect houses

4·800 m frontage

The medium frontage range of 4.800 m house types is suitable for densities between 175 ppha and 220 ppha, and offers a greater variety of layout solutions than its 3.600 m counterpart. The same distances (21.000 m and 12.000 m) between dwellings have to be observed as with the 3.600 m plans. Since the 4.800 m types are shallower than the 3.600 m, the gable walls will be less high when a normal pitched roof is used. The main advantage which the 4.800 m plans have over the narrow frontage plans is the width of the back garden, which in most cases is accessible from the living room.

In the layout illustrated, a variety of two-storey four, five and six person dwellings are shown with vehicular and pedestrian access in front of the house. There is also rear access to the back garden. A six person side-entry house (No. 4) gives elevational interest to an otherwise blank gable wall.

This 4.800 m type can be used in most layouts where a two-storey house is required, except in special situations where there may be a need for corner or controlled-aspect plans.

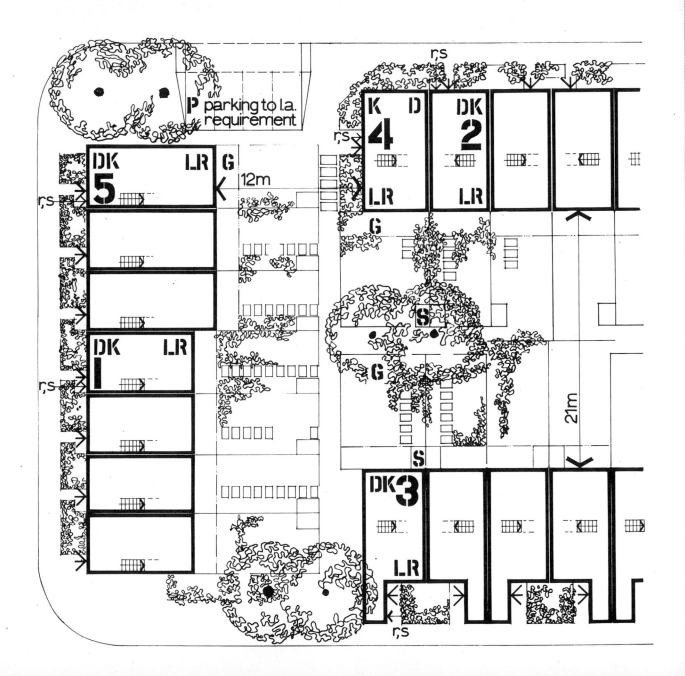

Layout implications
Dual aspect houses
4.800 m frontage

1

4 person 2 storey house
north/east/west entry
PDP 4199

2

5 person 2 storey house
north/east/west entry
PDP 5155

3

5 person 2 storey house
south entry
PDP 5162

4

6 person 2 storey house
side entry (5.400 m frontage)
PDP 6103

5

**6 person 2 storey
inter-terrace house**
north/east/west entry
PDP 6102

rs

refuse collection
service entry point

Scale

0   5   10

Dual aspect house

4·800 m frontage

This two-storey four person house can be planned in terraces with front door entry from north, east or west. The front door may be recessed to form a covered porch with a dustbin store if required.

The ground floor entrance hall serves the dining-kitchen and the living room. The staircase is next to the party wall. The two ground floor rooms are connected by double doors. The dining-kitchen area provides general storage units. The back garden is accessible from the living room. An external store of 2.000 m² is required, to conform to mandatory standards.

Upstairs there are one double bedroom and two single bedrooms, one of which is large enough to include general storage units. A bathroom is provided with separate WC. The central heating boiler is positioned next to the linen cupboard.

When planning the layout, the proximity of the public footpath to the front porch and kitchen window will be subject to the positioning of the dustbin store. The length of the back garden will be determined by the privacy distance required when dual–aspect dwellings back on to each other.

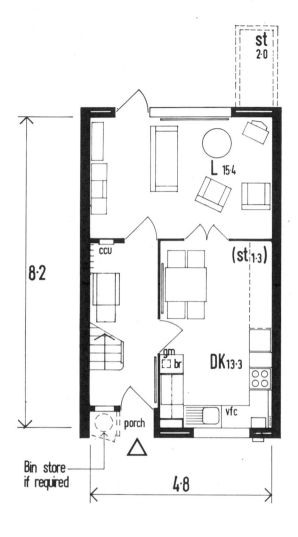

st
2·0

L 15·4

ccu

(st 1·3)

8·2

gm
br

DK 13·3

vfc

porch

Bin store
if required

4·8

GROUND FLOOR

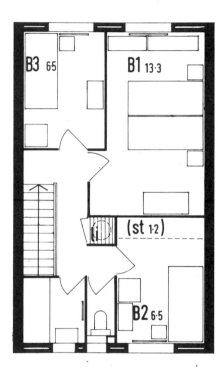

B3 6·5

B1 13·3

(st 1·2)

B2 6·5

FIRST FLOOR

PDP 4199
Dual aspect
2 storey house
4.800m frontage

4 person north entry type

Space (m²)		Mandatory	±%
Net	76·4	74·5	+2·5
Storage			
Int	2·5	4·5	
Ext	2·0		

Scale

0   1   2   3   4

PDP 5155

Dual aspect house

4·800 m frontage

This two-storey five person house can be planned in terraces with front door entry from north, east or west. The front door may be recessed to form a covered porch with a dustbin store if required.

The ground floor entrance hall serves the dining-kitchen, living room and WC. The staircase lies across the middle of the plan. The two ground floor rooms are connected by a door, with the option of building in storage at a later date. A broom cupboard is provided under the stair. Where the dwelling is located at the end of a terrace, an additional window to the dining-kitchen can be provided in the gable wall. The back garden is accessible from the living room. An external store of 2.300 m² is required, to conform to mandatory standards. The central heating boiler is positioned in the dining-kitchen area.

Upstairs there are two double bedrooms and one single bedroom, with bulkhead storage in one of the larger bedrooms. A bathroom is provided with combined WC.

When planning the layout, the proximity of the public footpath to the front porch and kitchen window will be subject to the positioning of the dustbin store. The length of the back garden will be determined by the privacy distance required when dual–aspect dwellings back on to each other.

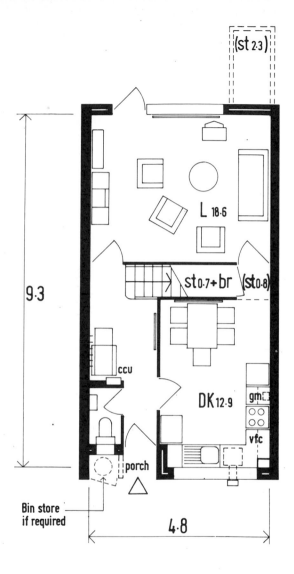

GROUND FLOOR

L 18·6

(st 2·3)

st 0·7 + br (st 0·8)

ccu

DK 12·9

gm

vfc

porch

Bin store
if required

9·3

4·8

FIRST FLOOR

B1 11·4

B3 6·1

st 0·7

B2 13·7

PDP 5155
Dual aspect
2 storey house
4.800m frontage

5 person north entry type

Space (m²)		Mandatory	±%
Net	85·6	85·0	+0·7
Storage			
Int	2·2	4·5	
Ext	2·3		

N

Scale

0   1   2   3   4

PDP 5162

Dual aspect house

4·800 m frontage

This two-storey five person house can be planned in terraces with front door entry from south, east or west. At the front of the house a single-storey entrance hall with a separate WC forms a projecting nib. A general store of 2.500 m² is required, to conform to mandatory standards. The single-storey projection may also include this general store and a dustbin shelter. The dwellings should be paired so that the adjoining nibs are combined under one roof, thereby minimising daylighting difficulties.

The ground floor entrance hall opens into the living room, which in turn leads into the dining room and kitchen. The dining-room and kitchen are connected by a door. The staircase lies across the middle of the plan and rises from the dining room. Access to the staircase from the entrance hall is through one end of the living room. The central heating boiler is positioned in the kitchen. Where the dwelling is located at the end of a terrace, an additional window to the living room can be provided in the gable wall. The back garden is accessible from the dining room.

Upstairs, a central landing serves two double bedrooms and one single bedroom, with bulkhead storage in one of the larger bedrooms. A bathroom is provided with combined WC. The linen cupboard is located on the landing.

When planning the layout, the public footpath in front of the house should not be less than 4.800 m from the living room window*. Within curtilage car parking can be provided in front of the living room. The length of the back garden will be determined by the privacy distance required when dual–aspect dwellings back on to each other.

*GLC standard.

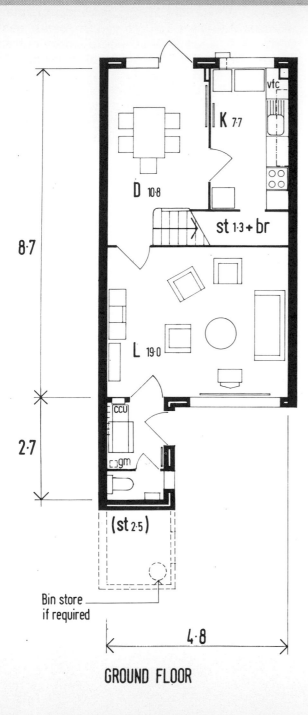

8·7

2·7

D 10·8

K 7·7

vfc

st 1·3 + br

L 19·0

CCU

gm

(st 2·5)

Bin store
if required

4·8

GROUND FLOOR

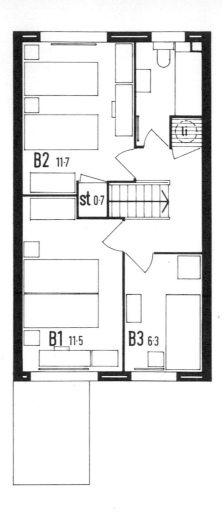

B2 11·7

st 0·7

B1 11·5

B3 6·3

FIRST FLOOR

·PDP 5162
Dual aspect
2 storey house
4·800m frontage

5 person south entry type

Space (m²)		Mandatory	±%
Net	85·6	85·0	+0·7
Storage			
Int	2·0	4·5	
Ext	2·5		

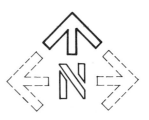

N

Scale

0   1   2   3   4

PDP 6102

Dual aspect house

4·800 m frontage

This two-storey six person house can be planned in terraces with front door entry from north, east or west. The front door may be recessed to form a covered porch with a dustbin store if required.

The ground floor entrance hall serves the dining-kitchen, living room and WC. The staircase is next to the party wall. The two ground floor rooms are connected by double doors, with the option of building in storage at a later date. The boiler is positioned centrally. Where the dwelling is located at the end of a terrace, an additional window to the dining-kitchen can be provided in the gable wall. The back garden is accessible from the living room.

Upstairs there are two double bedrooms and two single bedrooms, with storage space in one of the larger bedrooms. An internal mechanically–ventilated bathroom is provided with combined WC.

When planning the layout, the proximity of the public footpath to the front porch and kitchen window will be subject to the positioning of the dustbin store. The length of the back garden will be determined by the privacy distance required when dual–aspect dwelling back on to each other.

24

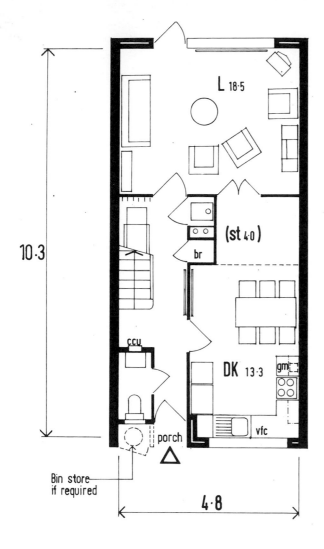

L 18·5

(st 4·0)

br

DK 13·3

gm

ccu

vfc

porch

Bin store
if required

10·3

4·8

GROUND FLOOR

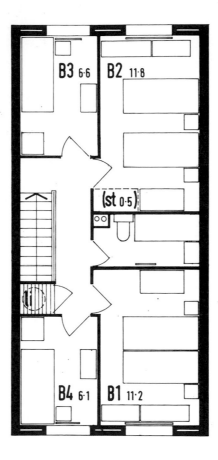

B3 6·6   B2 11·8

(st 0·5)

B4 6·1   B1 11·2

FIRST FLOOR

PDP 6102
Dual aspect
2 storey house
4.800m frontage

6 person north entry type

Space (m²)	Mandatory	±%
Net 93·2	92·5	+0·7
Storage 4·5	4·5	

Scale

0   1   2   3   4

Dual aspect houses

5·400 m frontage

The 5.400 m frontage range of plans is suitable for densities between 125 and 175 ppha. The range offers wider gardens and better room plans than the 4.800 m types. It also includes a south-entry plan without the projecting nib which is a dominant feature of the 4.800 m equivalent. The distances between dwellings (21.000 m and 12.000 m) are the same as those observed in the layouts of the other dual-aspect plans.

The layout illustrates the use of five different two-storey house types. All dwellings are accessible from the road in front. There is also access to the back gardens. The six person side entry house (No. 3) adds variety to an otherwise blank gable wall. The south-entry house types have slightly larger gardens than the rest of the plans, with garden access from the dining-kitchen.

The 5.400 m dual-aspect range fits well into most surburban situations.

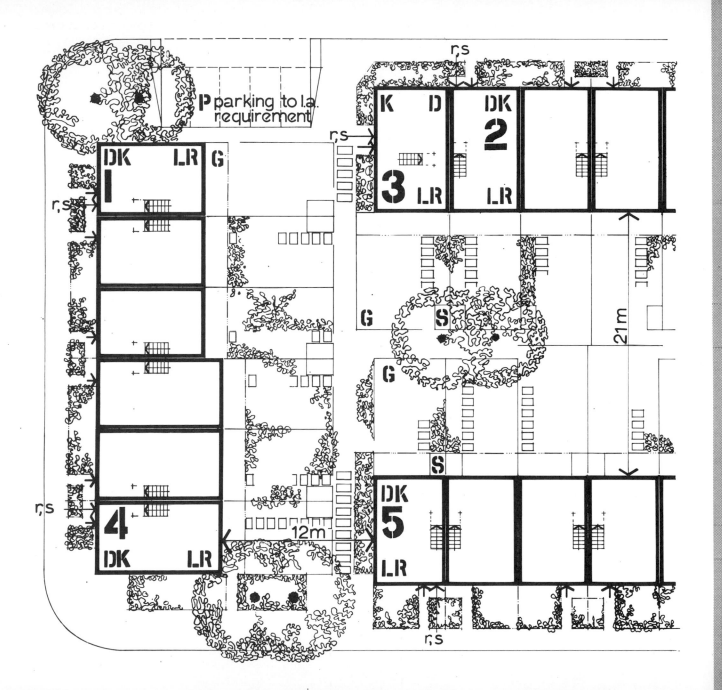

parking to l.a. requirement

r,s

12m

21m

Scale

0   5   10

PDP 5156

Dual aspect house

5·400 m frontage

This two-storey five person house can be planned in terraces with front door entry from north, east or west. The front door may be recessed to form a covered porch with a dustbin store if required.

The ground floor entrance hall serves the dining-kitchen, living room and WC. The staircase is next to the party wall. The two ground floor rooms are connected by double doors. The dining-kitchen area provides space for general storage and also houses the boiler. There is a built-in store under the staircase. Where the dwelling is located at the end of a terrace, an additional window to the dining-kitchen can be provided in the gable wall. The back garden is accessible from the living room.

Upstairs there are two double bedrooms and one single bedroom. Both double bedrooms are large enough to include space for general storage units. Additional bulkhead storage is built in over the staircase. A bathroom is provided with combined WC. The linen cupboard is located on the landing.

When planning the layout, the proximity of the public footpath to the front porch and kitchen window will be subject to the positioning of the dustbin store. The length of the back garden will be determined by the privacy distance required when dual–aspect dwellings back on to each other.

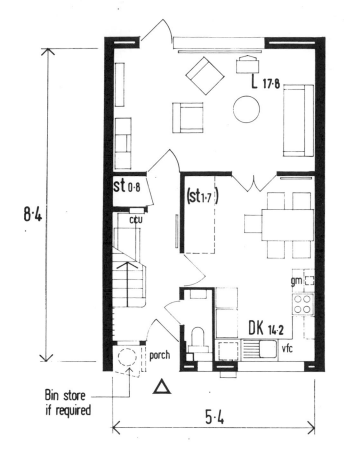

8·4

st 0·8

(st 1·7)

ccu

gm

DK 14·2

vfc

porch

Bin store
if required

△

5·4

L 17·8

GROUND FLOOR

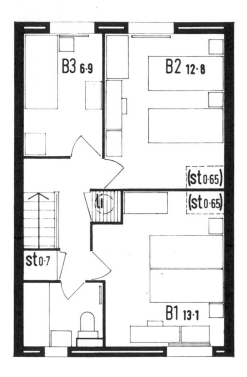

B3 6·9

B2 12·8

(st 0·65)

(st 0·65)

st 0·7

B1 13·1

FIRST FLOOR

PDP 5156
Dual aspect
2 storey house
5.400m frontage

5 person north entry type

Space (m²)		Mandatory	± %
Net	85·0	85·0	
Storage			
Int	4·5	4·5	

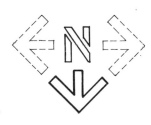

Scale

0   1   2   3   4

PDP 4201

Dual aspect house

5·400m frontage

This two-storey four person house can be planned in terraces with front door entry from south, east or west. The front door may be recessed to form a covered porch with a dustbin store if required.

The ground floor entrance hall serves the living room and dining-kitchen. The staircase is next to the party wall. The two ground floor rooms are connected by double doors. The dining-kitchen area provides space for general storage and also houses the boiler. The back garden is accessible from the dining-kitchen.

Two alternative plans are shown for the first floor, one with two double bedrooms, and one with a double and two single bedrooms. The bathroom, separate WC and linen cupboard with hot water cylinder are all accessible from the landing.

When planning the layout, the public footpath should not be less than 4.800 m from the living room window.* Within curtilage car parking can be provided in front of the living room. The length of the back garden will be determined by the privacy distance required when dual-aspect dwellings back on to each other.

*GLC standard.

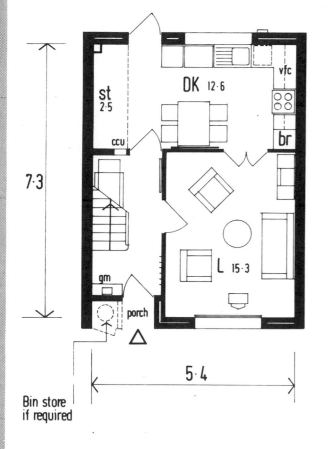

GROUND FLOOR

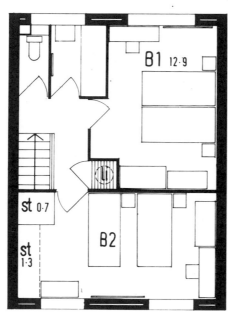

FIRST FLOOR
2 BEDROOMS

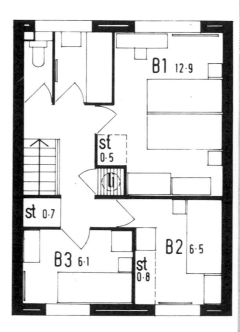

FIRST FLOOR
3 BEDROOMS

st 2·5

DK 12·6

vfc

ccu

br

7·3

L 15·3

gm

porch

5·4

Bin store
if required

B1 12·9

st 0·7

st 1·3

B2

B1 12·9

st 0·5

st 0·7

B3 6·1

st 0·8

B2 6·5

PDP 4201
Dual aspect
2 storey house
5·400 m frontage

4 person south entry type

Space (m²)	Mandatory	± %
Net 73·3	74·5	−1·5
Storage 4·5	4·5	

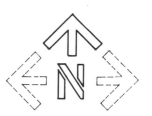

PDP 5157

Dual aspect house

5·400 m frontage

This two-storey five person house can be planned in terraces with front door entry from south, east or west. The front door may be recessed to form a covered porch with a dustbin store if required.

The ground floor entrance hall serves the living room, dining-kitchen, and WC. The staircase is next to the party wall. The two ground floor rooms are connected by double doors. The dining-kitchen area provides space for general storage and also houses the boiler. The back garden is accessible from the dining-kitchen.

Upstairs there are two double bedrooms and one single bedroom. Both double bedrooms are large enough to include space for general storage units. Additional bulkhead storage is built in over the staircase. A bathroom is provided with combined WC. The linen cupboard is located on the landing.

When planning the layout, the public footpath in front of the house should not be less than 4.800 m from the living room window*. Within curtilage car parking can be provided in front of the living room. The length of the back garden will be determined by the privacy distance required when dual–aspect dwellings back on to each other.

*GLC standard.

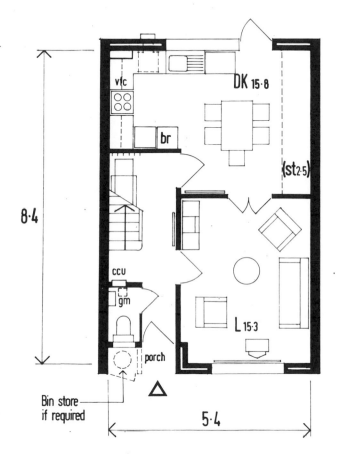

GROUND FLOOR

DK 15·8

vfc

br

(st 2·5)

ccu

gm

porch

L 15·3

8·4

5·4

Bin store
if required

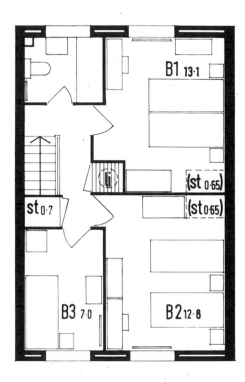

FIRST FLOOR

B1 13·1

st 0·7

(st 0·65)

(st 0·65)

B3 7·0

B2 12·8

PDP 5157
Dual aspect
2 storey house
5.400m frontage

5 person south entry type

Space (m²)		Mandatory	±%
Net	85·0	85·0	
Gen			
Storage	4·5	4·5	

Scale

0   1   2   3   4

Controlled aspect houses

5·400 m frontage

At densities between 120 and 175 ppha, there is also the option of using a 5.400 m medium frontage controlled-aspect type, where all habitable rooms are away from the entry side. With these plans, no habitable rooms need face each other, and this special arrangement enables the houses to be planned more closely together (at a minimum distance of 12.000 m instead of 21.000 m). Controlled-aspect plans also reduce the acceptable distance between the front of one house and the gable end of another.

In the layout illustrated, three different house types demonstrate the layout characteristics of controlled-aspect dwellings. The six person house (No. 3) with its two-storey nib presents a blank wall facing the gable wall of the terrace of five person dwellings. This enables the gap between the two terraces to be as narrow as possible. The first floor bedroom in the nib faces south and is not overlooked from any side. In the five person house (No. 2), the single-storey nib contains the kitchen only, and the positioning of the dwelling is less affected by overlooking problems.

Controlled-aspect dwellings can be used to narrow the ends of parallel terraces or to tighten up spaces which would otherwise not be enclosed.

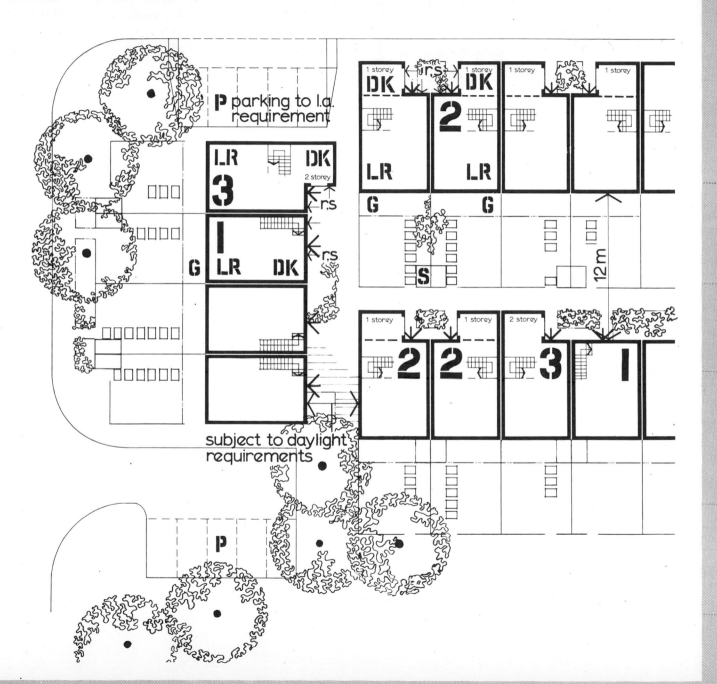

P parking to l.a. requirement

subject to daylight requirements

P

DK

3

LR DK
2 storey

G   LR   DK
r.s

1 storey   DK

DK
1 storey

LR
2
LR

G   G

S

12 m

1 storey   1 storey   2 storey

2   2   3   1

r.s

Layout implications
Controlled aspect houses
5.400 m frontage

1
4 person 2 storey house
north/east/west entry
PDP 4202

2
5 person 2 storey house
north/east/west entry
PDP 5158

3
6 person 2 storey house
north/east/west entry
PDP 6101

rs
refuse collection
service entry point

Scale

0   5   10

PDP 5158

Controlled aspect house

5·400 m frontage

This two-storey five person house can be planned in terraces with front door entry from north, east or west. The front door adjoins the projecting dining-kitchen and is overlooked from the kitchen window. A dustbin store may be positioned beside the entrance door if required.

The ground floor entrance hall serves the dining-kitchen, living room and single bedroom. A WC with hand washbasin adjoins the entrance door. The staircase lies across the middle of the plan. A broom cupboard is provided under the stair. The living room and dining-kitchen are connected by a door, with the option of building in storage at a later date. The central heating boiler is positioned in the kitchen. The back garden is accessible from the living room.

Upstairs, two double bedrooms face on to the back garden. The bulkhead linen cupboard and hot water cylinder open on to the landing and adjoin the combined bathroom and WC.

When planning the layout, the public footpath may be be hard up against the front wall of the house. The length of the back garden will be determined by the privacy distance required when dual–aspect dwellings back on to each other. Layouts based on the skilful use of this controlled-aspect type can overcome overlooking problems and can screen noise sources.

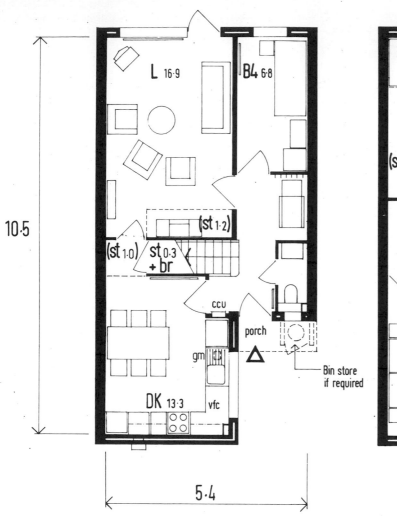

L 16·9   B4 6·8

(st 1·8)

(st 1·2)

(st 1·0)   st 0·3 + br

ccu

gm   porch

Bin store if required

DK 13·3   vfc

10·5

5·4

GROUND FLOOR

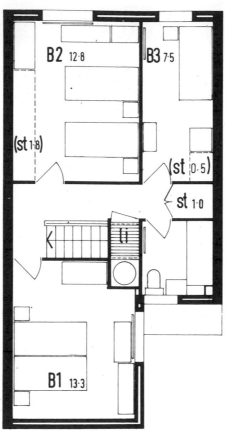

B2 12·8   B3 7·5

(st 0·5)

st 1·0

B1 13·3

FIRST FLOOR

PDP 5158
Controlled aspect
2 storey house
5.400m frontage

5 person north entry type

Space (m²)		Mandatory	±%
Net	84·2	85·0	−1·0
Storage	4·5		

Scale

0   1   2   3   4

PDP 6101

Controlled aspect house

5·400 m frontage

This two-storey six person house can be planned in terraces with front door entry from north, east or west. The front door adjoins the projecting dining-kitchen and is overlooked from the kitchen window. A dustbin store may be positioned beside the entrance door if required.

The ground floor entrance hall serves the dining-kitchen, living room and single bedroom. A WC with hand washbasin adjoins the entrance door. The staircase lies across the middle of the plan. The living room and dining–kitchen are connected by a door, with the option of building in storage at a later date. A broom cupboard is provided under the stairs. The central heating boiler is located in the kitchen. The back garden is accessible from the living room.

Upstairs there are two double bedrooms and one single bedroom. The bulkhead linen cupboard and hot water cylinder open on to the landing and adjoin the combined bathroom and WC.

When planning the layout, the public footpath may be hard up against the front wall of the house. The length of the back garden will be determined by the privacy distance required when dual–aspect dwellings back on to each other. Layouts based on the skilful use of this controlled-aspect type can overcome overlooking problems and can screen noise sources.

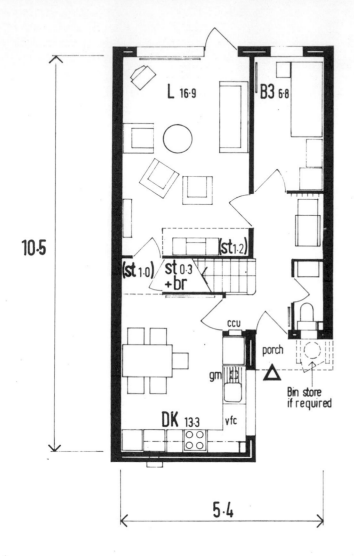

L 16·9   B3 6·8

(st 1·2)   st 0·3 +br   (st 1·0)

ccu   porch

gm   △   Bin store if required

DK 13·3   vfc

10·5

5·4

GROUND FLOOR

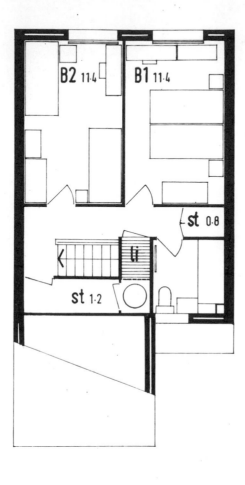

B2 11·4   B1 11·4

st 0·8

st 1·2   ti

FIRST FLOOR

PDP 6101
Controlled aspect
2 storey house
5.400m frontage

6 person north entry type

Space (m²)	Mandatory	±%
Net 93·7	92·5	+1·3
Storage		
Int 5·8	4·5	

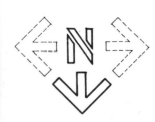

N

Scale

0   1   2   3   4

PDP
layout implications

Single aspect houses

over 6·600 m frontage

Wide frontage types of over 6.600 m have been developed for special sites where close proximity to motorways, railways or industry is likely to cause problems of noise and aspect. The increased width allows the dwellings to be planned with a single-aspect, so that all habitable rooms are restricted to one side of the plan. These types are of particular advantage in situations where footpaths pass close to front doors, or where the nearness of neighbouring dwellings can result in privacy problems. It is possible to build such dwellings very close together if required.

The layout illustrates the use of three different single-aspect plans. The grouping of dwellings is intimate and the enclosed spaces are small in scale. The space between the front walls of the four person and six person houses (Nos. 1 and 2) is of a minimum width and forms a pedestrian precinct, with shrubs and trees interspersed with paved areas. Private gardens are of more generous dimensions than can be achieved with the average terrace house.

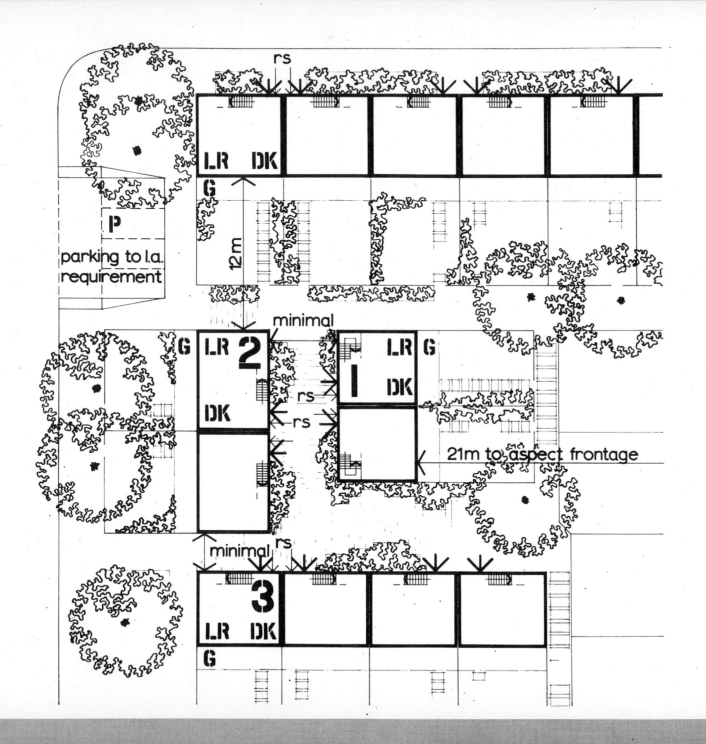

parking to l.a. requirement

P

rs

LR DK

G

12m

minimal

G LR **2**

DK

rs

rs

LR G

DK

1

21m to aspect frontage

minimal rs

LR **3** DK

G

Layout implications
Single aspect houses
Over 6.600 m frontage

1

4 person 2 storey house
north/east/west entry
PDP 4204

2

6 person 2 storey house
north/east/west entry
PDP 6104

3

5 person 2 storey house
north/east/west entry
PDP 5161

rs

refuse collection
service entry point

Scale

0   5   10

PDP 4204

Single aspect house

6·600 m frontage

This two-storey four person house can be planned in terraces with front door entry from north, east or west. The front door is located on the 'blind' side of the house. A dustbin store may be positioned beside the entrance door if required.

The ground floor entrance hall serves the dining-kitchen, living room and store beside the entrance door. The staircase rises along the 'blind' wall adjacent to the entrance door and projects into the living room, forming an angular encasement which can provide storage space if required. Provided that this storage space is not enclosed and that site conditions permit, a small window may be inserted into the 'blind' wall, allowing additional light into the living room. The garden is accessible from both the living room and the dining-kitchen. The central heating boiler is positioned in the dining-kitchen area.

Upstairs, one double bedroom and two single bedrooms face on to the back garden. The bathroom and adjacent separate WC are at the far end of the landing. The linen cupboard with the hot water cylinder is positioned outside bedroom 2 and is accessible from the landing.

When planning the layout, the public footpath may be hard up against the front wall of the house, subject to the positioning of the dustbin store. The length of the back garden will be determined by the privacy distance required when dual-aspect dwellings back on to each other. Layouts based on the skilful use of this single-aspect type can overcome overlooking problems and can screen noise sources.

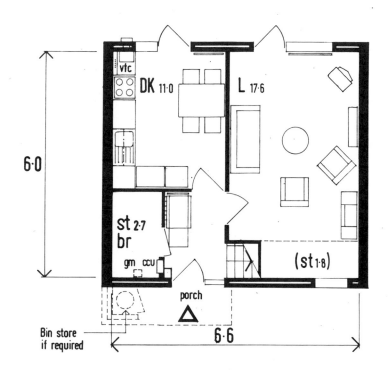

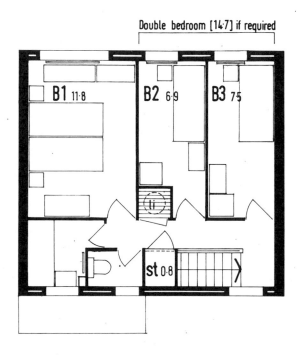

GROUND FLOOR

FIRST FLOOR

vtc

DK 11·0

L 17·6

st 2·7
br

gm ccu

(st 1·8)

6·0

porch

Bin store
if required

6·6

Double bedroom [14·7] if required

B1 11·8

B2 6·9

B3 7·5

st 0·8

PDP 4204
Single aspect
2 storey house
6.600m frontage

4 person north entry type

Space (m²)		Mandatory	±%
Net	74·7	74·5	+0·3
Storage	5·3	4·5	

Scale

0   1   2   3   4

PDP 5161

Single aspect house

7·200 m frontage

This two-storey five person house can be planned in terraces with front door entry from north, east or west. The front door is located on the 'blind' side of the house. A dustbin store may be positioned beside the entrance door if required.

The ground floor entrance hall serves the dining-kitchen, living room, WC and store. The staircase rises along the 'blind' wall adjacent to the entrance door and projects into the living room, forming an angular encasement which provides potential storage space. An external store of 2.200 m² is required, to conform to mandatory standards. A small window may be inserted into the 'blind' wall if site conditions permit, allowing additional light into the living room. The back garden is accessible from both the living room and the dining-kitchen. The central heating boiler is positioned in the dining-kitchen area.

Upstairs, two double bedrooms and one single bedroom face on to the back garden. The combined bathroom and WC is at the far end of the landing. A storage cupboard between bedrooms 1 and 3 is accessible from the landing. The linen cupboard and hot water cylinder adjoin the bathroom.

When planning the layout, the public footpath may be hard up against the front wall of the house, subject to the positioning of the dustbin store. The length of the back garden will be determined by the privacy distance required when dual-aspect dwellings back on to each other. Layouts based on the skilful use of this single-aspect type can overcome overlooking problems and can screen noise sources.

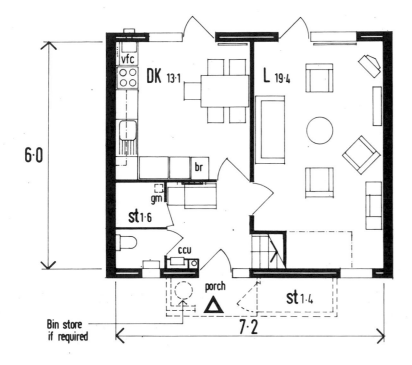

GROUND FLOOR

vfc
DK 13·1
L 19·4
br
gm
st 1·6
ccu
porch △
st 1·4
6·0
7·2
Bin store
if required

FIRST FLOOR

B1 11·2
B3 6·9
B2 10·8
st 0·7
st 0·8

PDP 5161
Single aspect
2 storey house
7.200m frontage

5 person north entry type

Space (m²)	Mandatory	±%
Net 84·0	85·0	−1·2
Storage		
Int 3·1		
Ext 1·4	4·5	

Scale

0   1   2   3   4

PDP 5159

135°
Corner
house

This two-storey five person corner house can be planned in terraces with front door entry from south, east or west. The front door is located on the living room side of the house in a recessed porch. The dustbin store may be positioned in the front porch or in the rear garden.

The ground floor entrance hall serves the dining-kitchen, living room and WC. The staircase is next to the party wall. General storage area has been provided in the dining-kitchen and in bedroom 3. The central heating boiler is situated under a worktop in the dining-kitchen, which opens on to the back garden.

Upstairs there are two double bedrooms and one single bedroom. The combined bathroom and WC faces the top of the stairs. The linen cupboard with the hot water cylinder adjoins the bathroom and is accessible from the landing.

When planning the layout, this corner solution can be used in conjunction with terraces of 5.400 m frontage south entry houses, provided that the depth of the houses is either the same as, or not less than 900 mm different from the depth of the adjacent dwellings. The front garden is overlooked by the living room and, due to the angular plan of the house, is of exceptional width. The layout of the back garden, with its diminishing width, requires special attention.

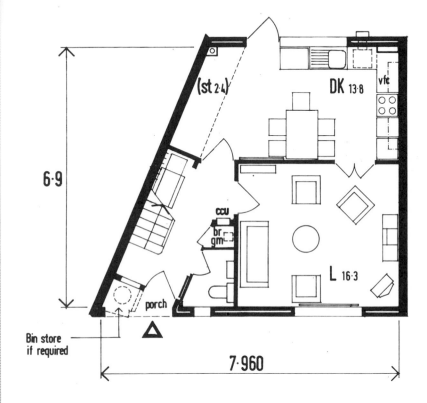

6·9

(st 2·4)

DK 13·8

vfc

ccu

br
gm

L 16·3

porch

Bin store
if required

△

7·960

GROUND FLOOR

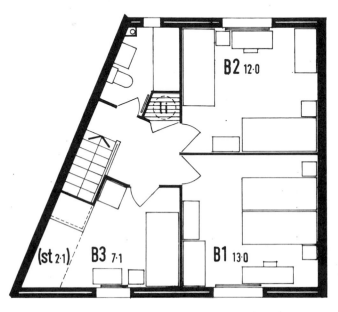

B2 12·0

(st 2·1)   **B3** 7·1   **B1** 13·0

FIRST FLOOR

PDP 5159
Dual aspect
2 storey house
135° corner

5 person south entry type

Space (m²)	Mandatory	±%
Net 84·6	85·0	−0·5
Storage 4·5	4·5	

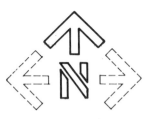

Scale

0   1   2   3   4

PDP
layout implications
2 storey flats

The illustration demonstrates the layout scope of the 6.000 m and 6.300 m frontage ranges of two person flats for two-storey terraces. Six different flat types have been used to produce the layout formation. The corner plans (Nos. 3, 4, 5) help to create a varied building form.

The side-entry type (No. 6) introduces some elevational interest to anotherwise blank gable wall, and has its living room facing west. The two adjacent north-entry types (No. 1) are paired and link up with a 6.300 m frontage internal corner type (No. 5), with living room and kitchen facing south. The adjoining pair of north-entry types (No. 1) then link up with an external corner dwelling (No. 3), which has its living room and bedroom facing east. The north-entry type which abuts it (No. 1) is paired with a south-entry type (No. 2). This arrangement overcomes the problem of overshadowing in the living room which would have been the case if a further north-entry type had been used.

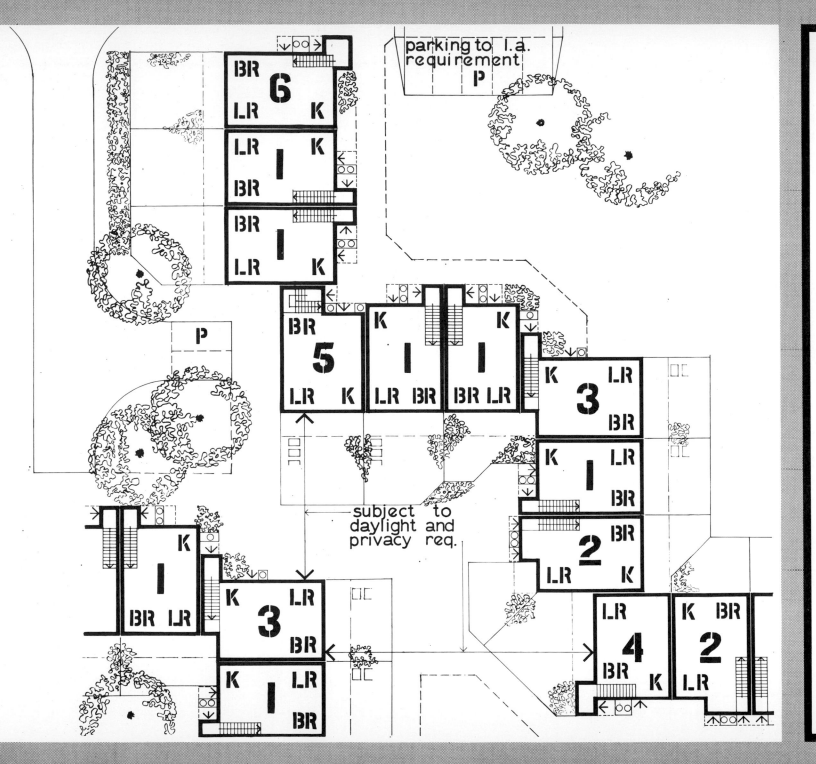

parking to l.a.
requirement
P

BR
6
LR K

LR K
I
BR

BR I
LR K

P

BR
5
LR K

K
I
LR BR

K
I
BR LR

K LR
3
BR

K
I
LR
BR

BR
2
LR K

subject to
daylight and
privacy req.

K
I
BR LR

K LR
3
BR
BR

K LR
I
BR

LR
4
BR K

K BR
2
LR

Layout implications
2 storey flats

1

2 person intermediate flat
north entry
PDP 2210

2

2 person intermediate flat
south entry
PDP 2207

3

2 person external corner flat
PDP 2209

4

2 person external corner flat
south entry
PDP 2224

5

2 person internal corner flat
PDP 2208

6

2 person flat
side entry
PDP 2225

N

Scale

0   5   10

2 storey flat

6·000 m frontage

This two person flat forms the ground floor and upper floor units in a two-storey block of flats, which can be planned in terraces with front door entry from the south.

The front door to the ground floor flat is positioned under a canopy which is an extension of the entrance lobby roof. This roof also shelters the dustbin enclosure and the projecting entrance to the upper flats. The ground floor flat has a small entrance hall with a broom cupboard, linen cupboard with hotwater cylinder and two small stores. The hall serves the living room, dining-kitchen, double bedroom and bathroom (1.500 m bath) with combined WC. The rear garden is accessible from the dining-kitchen.

The first floor flat has a small entrance lobby on the ground floor with a single flight stair along the party wall. The stair leads into a hall which serves the living room, double bedroom, kitchen, bathroom (1.500 m bath) with combined WC, linen cupboard with hot water cylinder and broom cupboard. Two stores are provided, one opening into the living room and one into the bedroom. Where flats are required to be individually heated, the plans can be modified to provide single boilers.

The flats conform to the standards specified for old people's dwellings. Ground floor flats also conform to mobility standards.

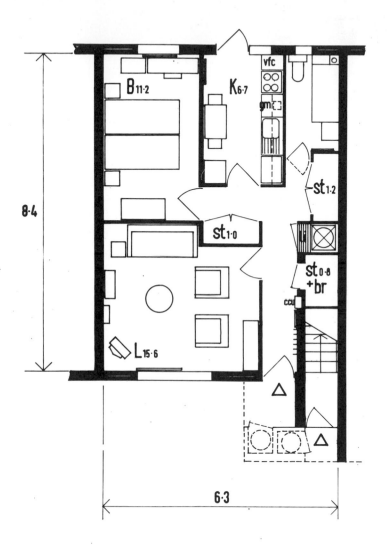

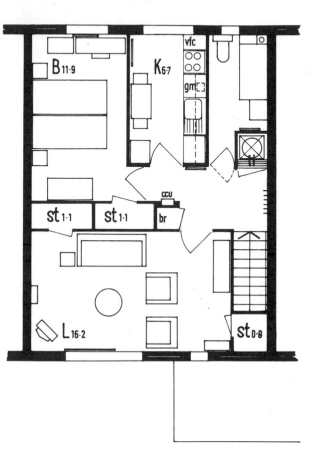

GROUND FLOOR FLAT

FIRST FLOOR FLAT

PDP 2207

2 storey flat
(enclosed stair)

2 person south entry type

Ground floor flat

Space (m²)	Mandatory	±%
Net 47·4	44·5	+6·5
Storage 3·0	3·0	

First floor flat

Space (m²)	Mandatory	±%
Net 47·6	44·5	+6·9
Storage 3·0	3·0	

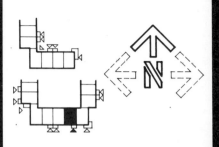

Scale

0   1   2   3   4

2 storey flat

6·300 m frontage

This two person flat forms the ground floor and upper floor units in a two-storey block of flats, and is intended for use in a 90° corner position where the block is flanked by adjacent terraces. The entrance to the flats is located on the inner corner.

The front door to the ground floor flat is positioned in a wide recess which also shelters the dustbin enclosure. The ground floor flat has an entrance hall which serves the living room, double bedroom, kitchen and bathroom (1.500 m bath) with combined WC. The garden is accessible from the living room. There is a linen cupboard with hot water cylinder in the hall, and a store accessible from the living room. The broom cupboard is located in the kitchen.

The first floor flat has a separate and recessed entrance lobby with dustbin enclosures on the ground floor, at right angles to the other entrance. A dog-legged staircase leads from the lobby to a landing, which in turn opens into a hall serving the living room, double bedroom, kitchen and combined bathroom and WC. There is a large store, a linen cupboard with hot water cylinder and a broom cupboard in the hall. A store is accessible from the living room. Where flats are required to be individually heated, the plans can be modified to provide single boilers.

The flats have their fenestration on adjacent walls, and assuming that the plans are mirrored, can be planned in layout positions with entry from north, east, west or south. The flats conform to the standards specified for old people's dwellings. Ground floor flats also conform to mobility standards.

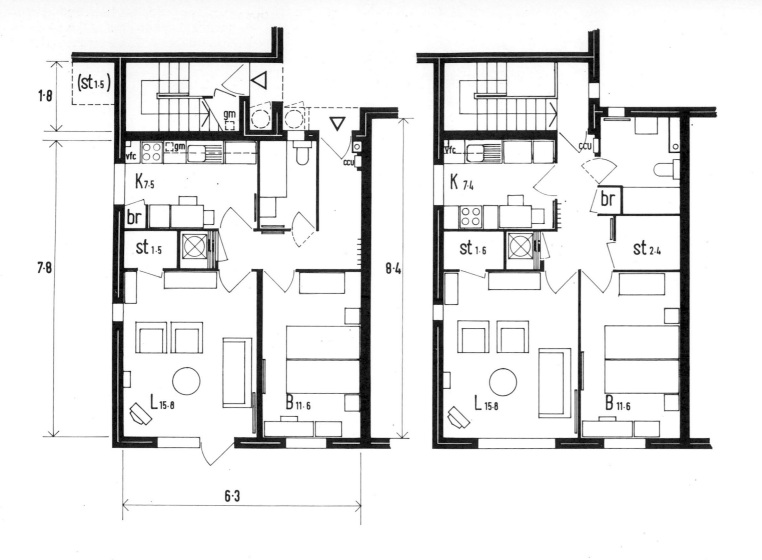

GROUND FLOOR FLAT

(st 1·5)

1·8

7·8

K 7·5

br

st 1·5

L 15·8

8·4

B 11·6

6·3

FIRST FLOOR FLAT

K 7·4

br

st 1·6

st 2·4

L 15·8

B 11·6

PDP 2208
2 storey flat
90° internal corner

2 person north entry type

Ground floor flat

Space (m²)	Mandatory	±%
Net 47·6	44·5	+6·9
Storage 3·0	3·0	

First floor flat

Space (m²)	Mandatory	±%
Net 48·7	44·5	+9·5
Storage 4·0	3·0	

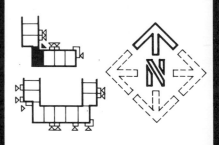

Scale

0   1   2   3   4

PDP 2209

2 storey flat

6·000 m frontage

This 8.400 m deep two person flat forms the ground floor and upper floor units in a two-storey block of flats, and is intended for use in a 90° corner position where the block is flanked by adjacent terraces. The entrance is located on the outer corner, at the side of the block.

The front door to the ground floor flat is positioned in a recess between the living room and the kitchen. The dustbin enclosure is outside the recess. The ground floor flat has an entrance hall which serves the dining-kitchen, living room, double bedroom, and bathroom with combined WC. A linen cupboard with hot water cylinder, and two stores are provided, all opening into the hall. The garden is accessible from the living room.

The first floor flat has a separate entrance beneath a projection along the gable wall of the flanking terrace. The entrance door is located under a canopy which extends over the dustbin enclosure. A single flight stair leads up to a landing which serves the dining-kitchen, living room, double bedroom, bathroom with combined WC, linen cupboard with hot water cylinder, and store. Where flats are required to be individually heated, the plans can be modified to provide single boilers.

The flats have their fenestration on adjacent walls, and assuming that the plans are mirrored, can be planned in layout positions with entry from north, east, west or south. The flats conform to the standards specified for old people's dwellings. Ground floor flats also conform to mobility standards.

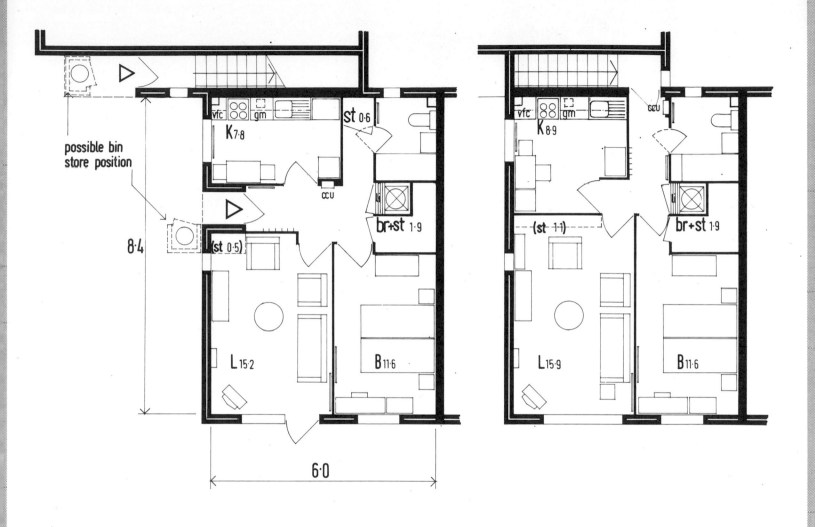

possible bin
store position

8·4

K 7·8

vfc   gm

st 0·6

ccu

br+st 1·9

(st 0·5)

L 15·2

B 11·6

6·0

GROUND FLOOR FLAT

K 8·9

vfc   gm

ccu

(st 1·1)

br+st 1·9

L 15·9

B 11·6

FIRST FLOOR FLAT

PDP 2209
2 storey flat
90° external corner

2 person north entry type

Ground floor flat

Space (m²)		Mandatory	±%
Net	46·2	44·5	+3·8
Storage	3·5	3·0	

First floor flat

Space (m²)		Mandatory	±%
Net	49·2	44·5	+10·5
Storage	3·0	3·0	

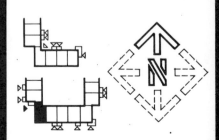

Scale

0   1   2   3   4

2 storey flat

6·000 m frontage

This two person flat forms the ground floor and upper floor units in a two-storey block of flats, which can be planned in terraces with front door entry from north, east or west.

The front door to the ground floor flat is positioned under a deep canopy which extends over the dustbin enclosures and the projecting entrance lobby to the upper flat. The ground floor flat has an entrance hall which serves the living room, double bedroom, kitchen, combined bathroom (1.500 m bath) and WC and store. When the flat is located in an end of terrace position, an additional small window may be provided in the gable wall to allow extra light into the living room. The garden is accessible from the living room.

The first floor flat has a separate entrance lobby with a single flight stair along the party wall. The stair leads into a hall which serves the living room, double bedroom and combined bathroom (1.500 m bath) and WC. The kitchen is accessible from the living room. Two small stores are provided, which open into the hall. Where flats are required to be individually heated, the plans can be modified to provide single boilers.

The flats conform to the standards specified for old people's dwellings. Ground floor flats also conform to mobility standards.

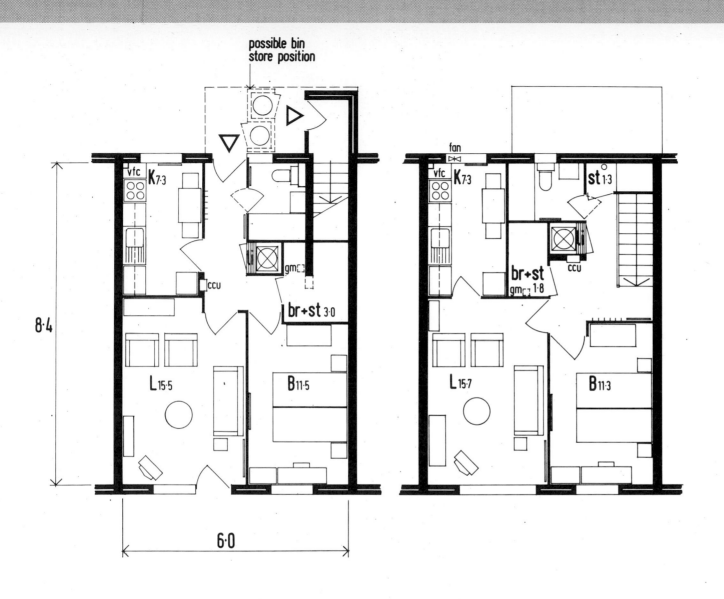

possible bin
store position

vfc K7·3

ccu

br+st 3·0

gm

8·4

L 15·5

B 11·5

6·0

GROUND FLOOR FLAT

fan

vfc K7·3

st 1·3

br+st
gm 1·8

ccu

L 15·7

B 11·3

FIRST FLOOR FLAT

PDP 2210
2 storey flat
enclosed stair

2 person north-entry type

Ground floor flat

Space (m²)		Mandatory	± %
Net	44·8	44·5	+0·7
Storage	3·0	3·0	.

First floor flat

Space (m²)		Mandatory	± %
Net	45·1	44·5	+1·3
Storage	3·1	3·0	

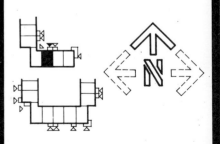

Scale

0   1   2   3   4

PDP 2224

2 storey flat

6·300 m frontage

This 8.400 m deep two person flat forms the ground floor and upper floor units in a two-storey block of flats, and is intended for use in a 90° corner position where the block is flanked by adjacent terraces. The entrance is located on the outer corner at the front of the block, providing a wide garden at the side.

The front door to the ground floor flat is positioned under a canopy which extends over the dustbin enclosures and the projecting entrance lobby to the upper flat. The ground floor flat has an entrance hall which serves the living room, double bedroom, kitchen and bathroom (1.500 m bath) with combined WC. A small store under the stairs to the flat above adjoins the front door, and there is an additional store opening into the hall, as well as a linen cupboard with hot water cylinder. The garden is accessible from the living room.

The first floor flat has a small projecting entrance lobby on the ground floor with a single flight of stairs leading into the hall. The disposition of rooms is identical to the flat below, with the exception of a small bulkhead store in the bedroom which replaces the entrance hall store in the ground floor flat. Where flats are required to be individually heated, the plans can be modified to provide single boilers.

The flats have their fenestration on adjacent walls, and assuming that the plans are mirrored, can be planned in layout positions with entry from north, east, west or south. The flats conform to the standards specified for old people's dwellings. Ground floor flats also conform to mobility standards.

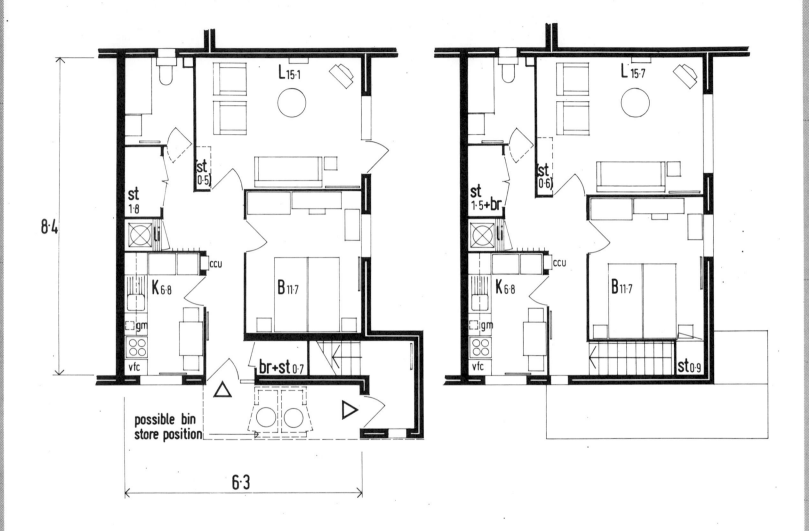

GROUND FLOOR FLAT

FIRST FLOOR FLAT

Ground floor flat labels:
L 15·1, st (0·5), st 1·8, K 6·8, gm, vfc, ccu, B 11·7, br+st 0·7

possible bin
store position

8·4

6·3

First floor flat labels:
L 15·7, st (0·6), st 1·5+br, K 6·8, gm, vfc, ccu, B 11·7, st 0·9

PDP 2224
2 storey flat
90° external corner

2 person south entry type

Ground floor flat

Space (m²)		Mandatory	±%
Net	47·4	44·5	+6·8
Storage	3·0	3·0	

First floor flat

Space (m²)		Mandatory	±%
Net	48·1	44·5	+8·1
Storage	3·0	3·0	

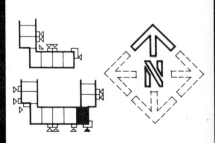

Scale

0   1   2   3   4

PDP 2225

2 storey flat

6·000 m frontage

This two person flat forms the ground floor and upper floor units in a two-storey block of flats, which can be planned in an end of terrace position where side entry is required. Front door entry can be from north, east or south and if the plans are mirrored, from the west.

The front door to the ground floor flat is positioned under a canopy which extends over the dustbin enclosures and the projecting entrance lobby to the upper flat. The ground floor flat has an entrance hall which serves the living room, double bedroom, combined bathroom (1.500 m bath) and WC and store. The kitchen is accessible from the living room, which opens on to the garden.

The first floor flat has a separate entrance lobby with a single flight stair along the gable wall. The stair leads into a hall which serves the living room, double bedroom and combined bathroom (1.500 m bath) and WC. The kitchen is accessible from the living room. Two small stores are provided, which open into the hall. Where flats are required to be individually heated the plans can be modified to provide single boilers.

The flats conform to the standards specified for old people's dwellings. Ground floor flats also conform to mobility standards.

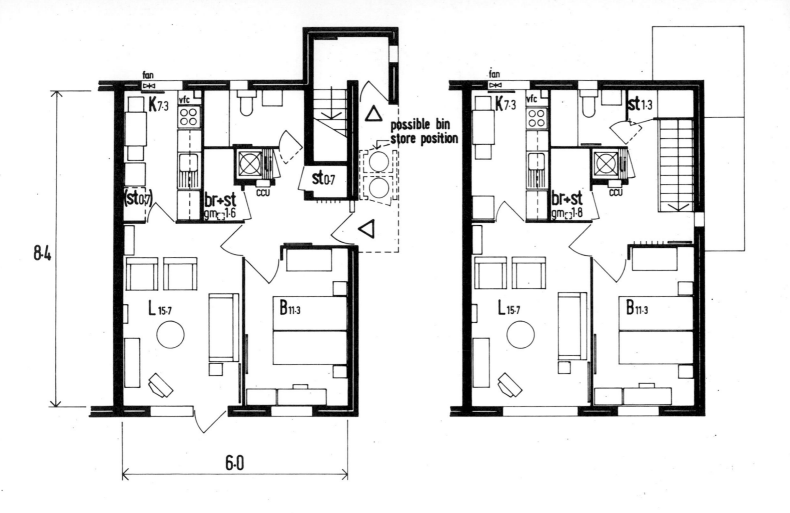

GROUND FLOOR FLAT

FIRST FLOOR FLAT

fan

K 7.3   vfc

(st 0.7)

br+st
gm 1.6

CCU

st 0.7

possible bin
store position

L 15.7

B 11.3

8.4

6.0

fan

K 7.3   vfc

st 1.3

br+st
gm 1.8

CCU

L 15.7

B 11.3

PDP 2225

2 storey flat
(enclosed stair)

2 person end entry type

Ground floor flat

Space (m²)		Mandatory	±%
Net	44.8	44.5	+0.7
Storage	3.0	3.0	

First floor flat

Space (m²)		Mandatory	±%
Net	45.1	44.5	+1.3
Storage	3.1	3.0	

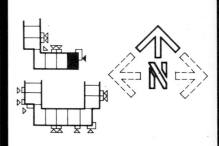

Scale

0   1   2   3   4

3 storey flat

6·300 m frontage

This two person flat forms the ground floor, first and second floor units in a three-storey block of flats with front door entry from north, east or west. A shared dog-legged staircase serves four flats, two on the first floor and two on the second. The plans of the flats are virtually identical and are mirrored when positioned on either side of the staircase. A canopy can be provided to give covered access to those refuse stores serving old people's dwellings.

The front door to each of the flats is in a similar position, but the approaches to the flats vary. Each of the ground floor flats has an individual entrance with a porch. An electrical intake and distribution cupboard is located at the side of one of the porches. To satisfy CP3 fire regulation requirements, the first floor flats are entered through a smoke lobby, separated from the staircase by a door with a vision panel. The lobby is lit by a window in the outside wall. In the case of the second floor flats, the separating door is not required.

The entrance hall serves the living room, double bedroom, combined bathroom (1.500 m bath) and WC, and linen cupboard containing the hot water cylinder and cold water tank. The kitchen is accessible from the living room. The main store opens into the living room. A further store is located in the kitchen and optional stores are in the hall, bedroom and living room. The living room in the ground floor flats opens on to the garden. Heating is provided from a central heating boiler which serves a number of blocks.

The ground floor and first floor flats conform to the standards specified for old people's dwellings. Ground floor flats also conform to mobility standards.

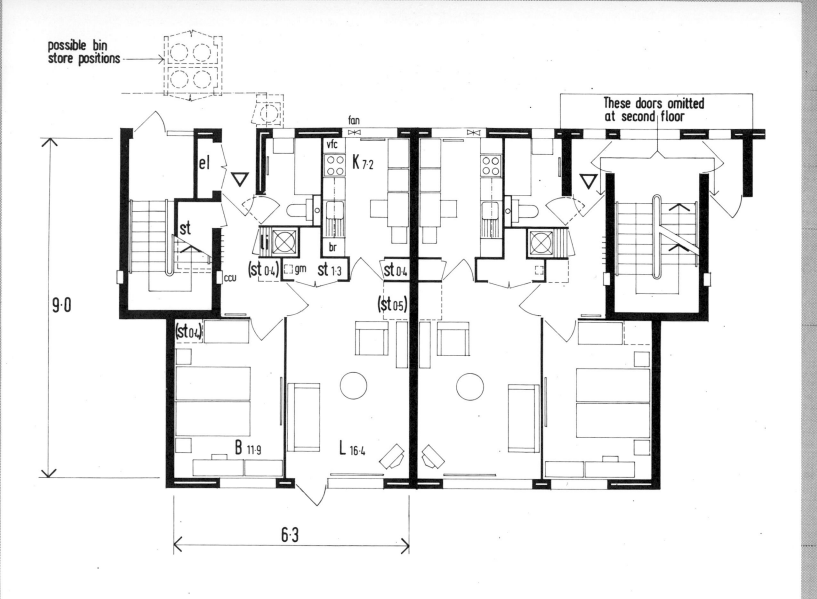

possible bin
store positions

These doors omitted
at second floor

9·0

el

st

ccu

(st 0·4)

vfc

K 7·2

li

(st 0·4)   gm   st 1·3   st 0·4

br

(st 0·5)

fan

B 11·9   L 16·4

6·3

GROUND FLOOR FLAT

FIRST & SECOND FLOOR FLATS

PDP2211
3 storey flat

2 person north entry type

Space (m²)	Mandatory	±%
Net 45·8	44·5	+2·9
Storage		
Int 3·0	3·0	

Scale

0   1   2   3   4

PDP 2212

3 storey flat

6·500 m frontage

This two person flat forms the ground floor, first and second floor units in a three-storey block of flats with front door entry from the south. A shared dog-legged staircase serves four flats, two on the first floor and two on the second. The plans of the flats are vitually identical and are mirrored when positioned on either side of the staircase. A canopy can be provided to give covered access to those refuse stores serving old people's dwellings.

The front door to each of the flats is in a similar position, but the approaches to the flats vary. Each of the ground floor flats has an individual entrance with a porch. An electrical intake and distribution cupboard is located at the side of one of the porches. To satisfy CP3 fire regulation requirements, the first floor flats are entered through a smoke lobby, separated from the staircase by a door with a vision panel. In the case of the second floor flats, the separating door is not required.

The entrance hall serves the living room, double bedroom, kitchen, combined bathroom and WC, and linen cupboard containing the hot water cylinder and cold water tank. There are three stores accessible from the hall, the bedroom and the living room respectively, and an additional optional store in the bedroom. Heating is provided from a central heating boiler which serves a number of blocks.

The ground floor and first floor flats conform to the standards specified for old people's dwellings. Ground floor flats also conform to mobility standards.

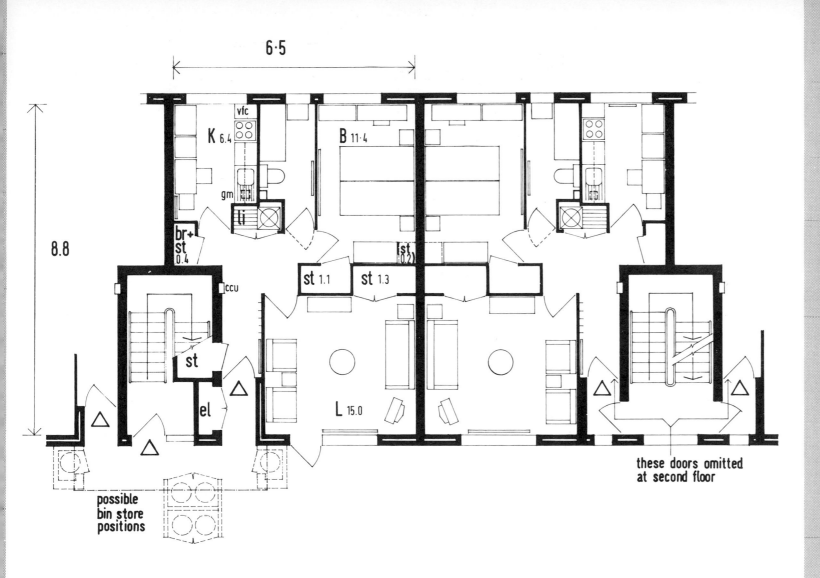

6·5

8·8

K 6.4

vfc

B 11·4

gm

li

br+ st 0.4

ccu

st

el

st 1.1

st 1.3

st (0.2)

L 15.0

possible bin store positions

these doors omitted at second floor

GROUND FLOOR FLAT

FIRST & SECOND FLOOR FLATS

PDP 2212
3 storey flat

2 person south entry type

Space (m²)	Mandatory	± %
Net 46·3	44·5	+4·0
Storage		
Int 3·0	3·0	

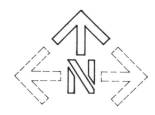

N

Scale

0   1   2   3   4

PDP 2218

3 storey corner flat

This 9.000 m deep two person flat forms the ground floor, first and second floor units in a three-storey block of flats, and is intended for use in a 135° corner position where the block is flanked by adjacent terraces. Front door entry can be from north, east or west. A shared dog-legged staircase serves four flats, two on the first floor and two on the second. The plans of the flats are virtually identical and are mirrored when positioned on either side of the staircase. A canopy can be provided to give covered access to those refuse stores serving old people's dwellings.

The front door to each of the flats is in a similar position, but the approaches to the flats vary. Each of the ground floor flats has an individual entrance with a porch. An electrical intake and distribution cupboard is located at the side of one of the porches. To satisfy CP3 fire regulation requirements, the first floor flats are entered through a smoke lobby, separated from the staircase by a door with a vision panel. In the case of the second floor flats, the separating door is not required.

The entrance hall serves the living room, double bedroom, kitchen, combined bathroom (1.500 m bath) and WC, and linen cupboard containing the hot water cylinder and cold water tank. There are three stores accessible from the hall, the kitchen and the living room respectively. The living room in the ground floor flats opens on to the garden. Heating is provided from a central heating boiler which serves a number of blocks.

The ground floor and first floor flats conform to the standards specified for old people's dwellings. Ground floor flats also conform to mobility standards.

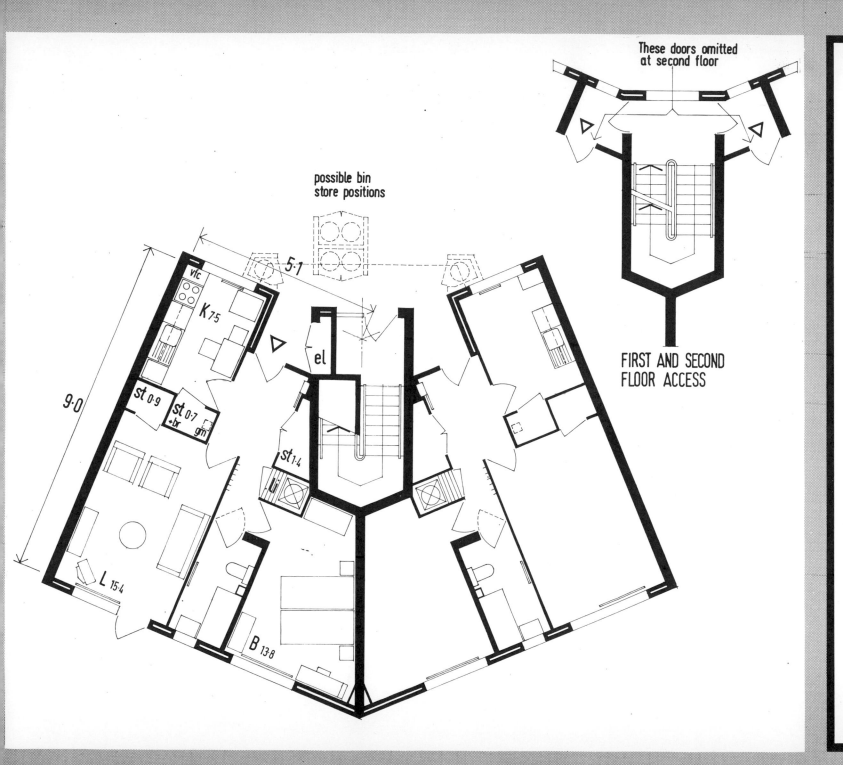

These doors omitted
at second floor

possible bin
store positions

5·1

9·0

v/c

K 7·5

el

st 0·9

st 0·7
+br
gm

st 1·4

L 15·4

B 13·8

FIRST AND SECOND
FLOOR ACCESS

PDP 2218
3 storey flat
135° internal corner

2 person north entry type

Space (m²)		Mandatory	±%
Net	48·5	44·5	+11·1
Storage	3·0	3·0	

Scale

0   1   2   3   4

Layout theory

Example 1

Layout example 1 demonstrates the use of a small cluster of PDPs on a pedestrian courtyard development. The layout is based on a density of 200 ppha with 90 per cent car parking provision. The landscaped central precinct measures approximately 15.000 m by 35.000 m (the larger dimension depending upon the permitted carry distance between the service points) and is surrounded by two-storey houses and flats. As the entrances to all the dwellings face the central area, casual supervision by residents should prevent damage to common property. Service points and car parking areas are located at the northern and southern edges of the pedestrian precinct.

The narrow northern end of the courtyard is partially enclosed by a block of south-entry old people's flats, entered via a front garden which acts as a privacy zone in front of living room windows. Since the flats overlook the central area, there is plentiful contact with the neighbouring community. The western side of the courtyard is formed by a terrace of dual-aspect houses, with entrances next to the kitchen windows. The eastern side consists of a terrace of flats with living rooms and bedrooms facing east, away from the pedestrian area. This arrangement allows the distance between the entrances to the flats and the dwellings on the opposite side to be less than the normally required 21.000 m. On the southern flank of the courtyard, a series of dual-aspect staggered houses steps up the slope leading to the pedestrian precinct. The near closure effect at the western junction is formed by a single-aspect house. The walk-through to the north-western corner of the courtyard is similarly lined by a row of stepped and staggered dual-aspect houses which lead down to further clusters of housing beyond.

Introduction
The PDP range has been designed to answer a number of important layout criteria relating to density, assimilation into the existing environment and car accommodation. The scale of the plans and their inter-relationships have been chosen with a view to producing an identifiable sense of place in the spaces which they enclose.

The following examples illustrate the layout potential of PDPs on three theoretical schemes and four actual sites.

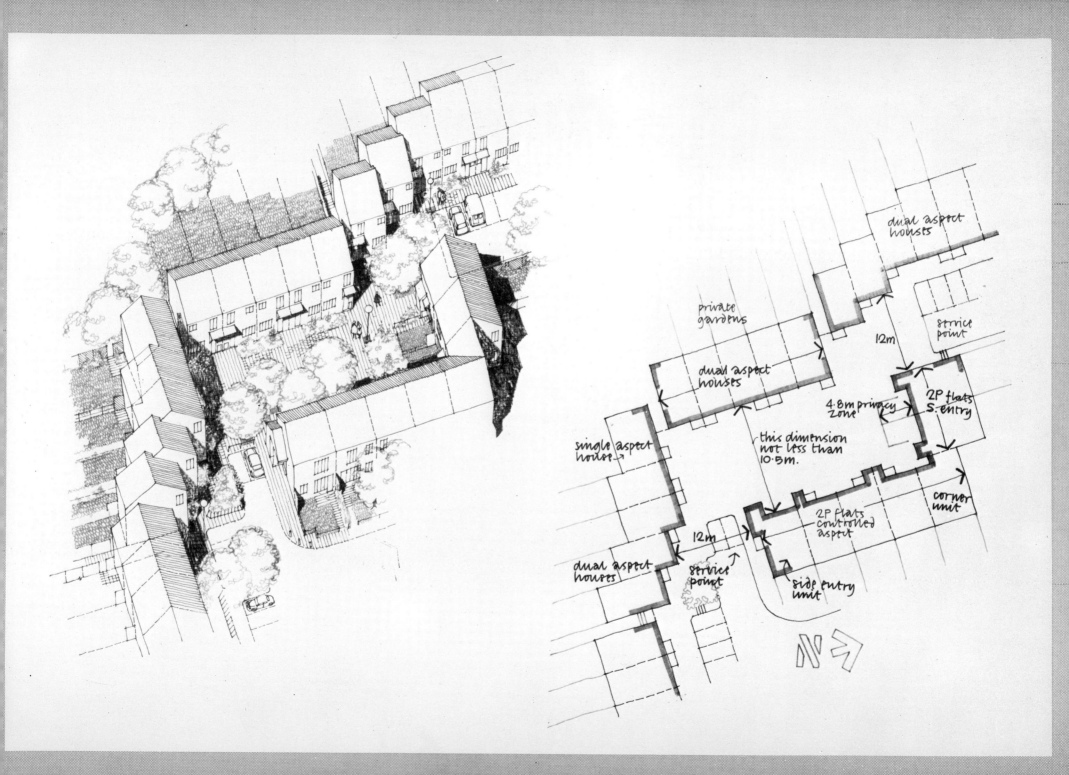

private
gardens

dual aspect
houses

dual aspect
houses

single aspect
house →

this dimension
not less than
10·5m.

4·8m privacy
zone

12m

service
point

2P flats
S·entry

2P flats
controlled
aspect

corner
unit

12m

dual aspect
houses

service
point

side entry
unit

Layout theory

Example 2

The second layout example also takes the form of a cluster, but as it forms part of a large scheme which calls for pedestrian movement to the east, its orientation is different. The layout is based on a density of 175 ppha with 70 per cent car parking provision. As in the previous layout, all front doors face the courtyard, or in this case mews, and casual supervision by residents should minimise the risk of vandalism. The dimensions of the central courtyard are approximately 25.000 m by 50.000 m and the area is enclosed by two-storey houses. In contrast to example 1 where the central area was totally pedestrian, this mews type of cluster contains service points and car parking within its enclosed space and is therefore somewhat different in character.

The road enters the cluster in the south-western corner, through a 12.000 m gap between two terraces of dual-aspect houses. If the east-facing windows of the corner house of the western terrace were moved to the gable wall, the width of this gap could be reduced. The projection of the controlled-aspect house between the northern and western flank narrows the gap at this point and helps to turn the corner. The projection can be either single-storey or two-storey, depending on whether a five or six person house is required. The northern side of the mews is bordered by a terrace of twelve south-entry dual-aspect houses with single-storey projections and 4.800 m privacy zones in front of living room windows. The eastern end of the cluster narrows into a gap of about 6.000 m which links the main pedestrian route with a further series of housing clusters. The narrowing at this point has been achieved with stepped and staggered south-entry dual-aspect houses on the northern side and similarly arranged controlled-aspect houses on the southern side, where the pitched roofs of the houses inter-penetrate each other. The southern flank of the mews continues with a terrace of dual-aspect houses leading up to the road entry point.

Some in-curtilage car parking is provided in front of the dual-aspect houses on the southern and western sides of the mews. Parking spaces are grouped together and cut into the rising ground. Heavy planting and hard landscaping around the parking areas, which are partly about 0.500 m below pedestrian level, help to subdue the impact of the car. The treatment of the road surface can be changed beyond the service point at the eastern end of the mews.

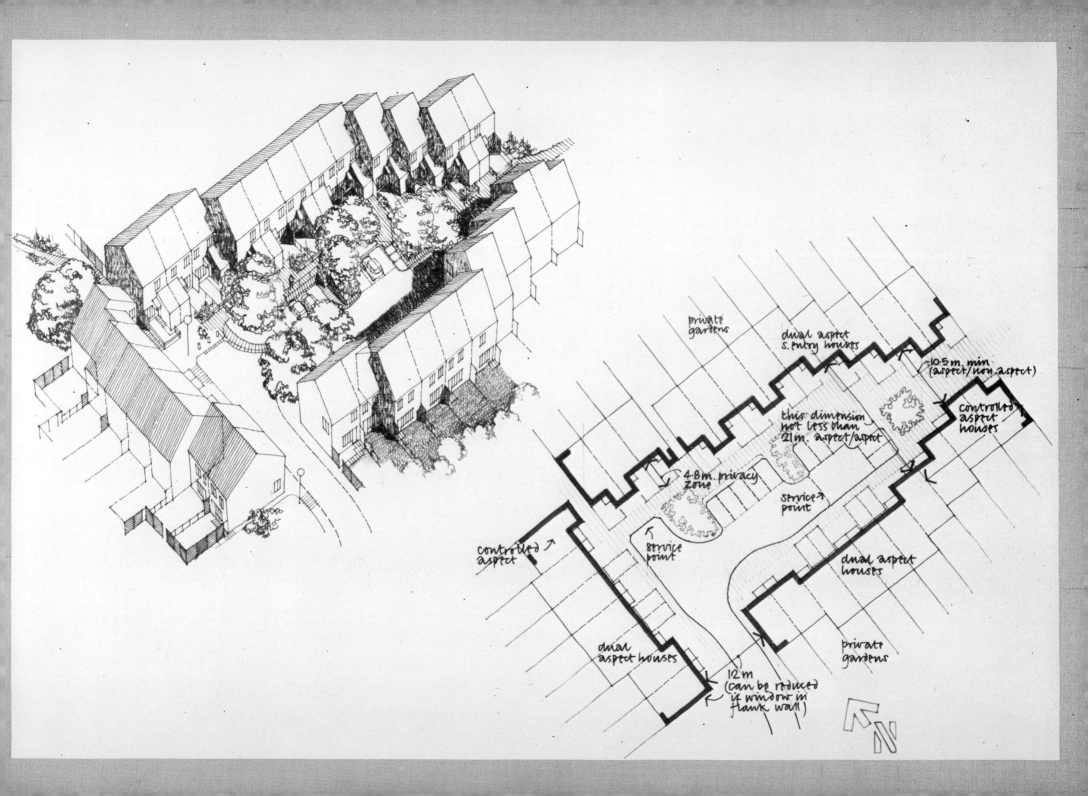

private gardens

dual aspect
s. entry houses

10·5 m. min
(aspect/non aspect)

controlled
aspect
houses

this dimension
not less than
21 m. aspect/aspect

4·8 m. privacy
zone

service
point

controlled
aspect

service
point

dual aspect
houses

dual
aspect houses

private
gardens

12 m
(can be reduced
if window in
flank wall)

N

Layout theory
Example 3

As in the previous layout example, the dwellings have been clustered round a central pedestrian/vehicular courtyard. The layout uses a mix of two person flats and family houses to achieve a density of about 225 ppha with 90 per cent car parking provision. Vehicular and pedestrian access to the courtyard is from the north, and a secondary footpath system which links the cluster with further areas of housing is connected to the court at the south-western corner. To accommodate the number of cars required and to provide adequate turning space for service vehicles, the dimensions of the parking court exceed 21.000 m, ensuring sufficient privacy distances for a high proportion of dual-aspect houses to be used.

The northern and eastern sides of the courtyard are enclosed by terraces of two-storey flats, linked by a closed corner unit to form an L-shaped block. The living rooms of the south-entry flats on the eastern side overlook the central area. Low fenced private gardens 4.800 m deep in front of the flats, ensure that privacy is maintained. On the southern and western sides, the courtyard is bordered by dual-aspect family houses. At the south-east and south-west corners, controlled-aspect houses form narrow bottlenecks through which the footpath link enters and leaves the courtyard, providing a strong sense of visual enclosure while maintaining privacy.

Landscaping and changes of level reduce the visual impact of the central parking area, as in the last example. In-curtilage parking is provided for a proportion of family houses.

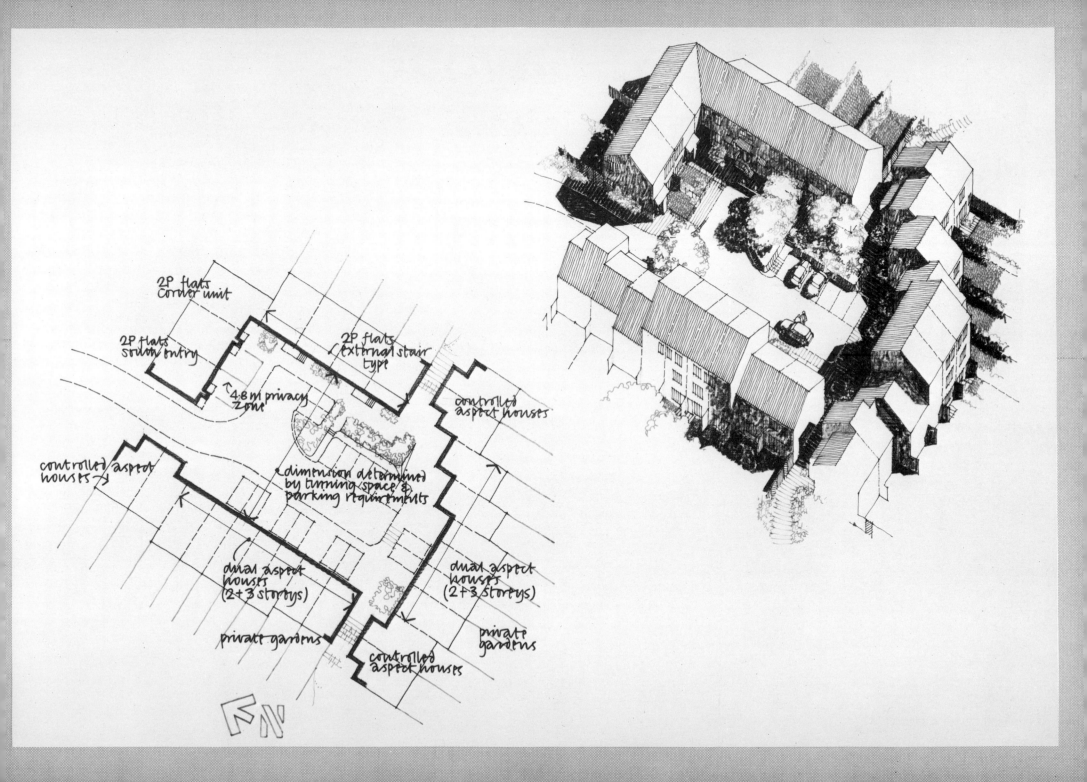

2P flats
corner unit

2P flats
south entry

2P flats
external stair
type

4.8 m privacy
zone

controlled
aspect houses

controlled aspect
houses

dimension determined
by turning space &
parking requirements

dual aspect
houses
(2 + 3 storeys)

dual aspect
houses
(2 + 3 storeys)

private gardens

controlled
aspect houses

private
gardens

N

Layout practice

Benhilton Gardens

This 0.4 ha site is triangular and slopes sharply uphill from the entry point towards the north-eastern corner. The eastern part of the side has been left free of buildings, in order to perserve the many mature trees.

The layout comprises four blocks of two-storey two person flats, providing a total of 31 old people's dwellings, along with eight car parking spaces. The flats are laid out in terraces and have individual entrances at ground floor level. Road access is from the south and leads to a centrally located service point. A series of steps rises from the service point to the entrances of the flats to blocks 2 and 3. The kitchens and bathrooms of these flats face each other on the access side, allowing the blocks to be positioned in close proximity. The living rooms overlook the eastern and western parts of the site. At the upper end of block 2 is a single-storey boiler house containing the gas-fired district heating. At the southern end of block 3 on the ground floor, there is a clubroom. Block 1 is approached by a shallow ramp and consists of a terrace terminated at the far end by a 90° corner unit (PDP 2208), with a dog-leg staircase against the flanking wall of the adjacent flats. Block 4 is approached by a level walkway.

With the exception of the block 1 corner unit, all the flats are based on PDP 2210. Private gardens are positioned away from access routes, providing maximum privacy. A few dwellings have been stepped and staggered to overcome the critical sunlight problems caused by the steep slope of the site.

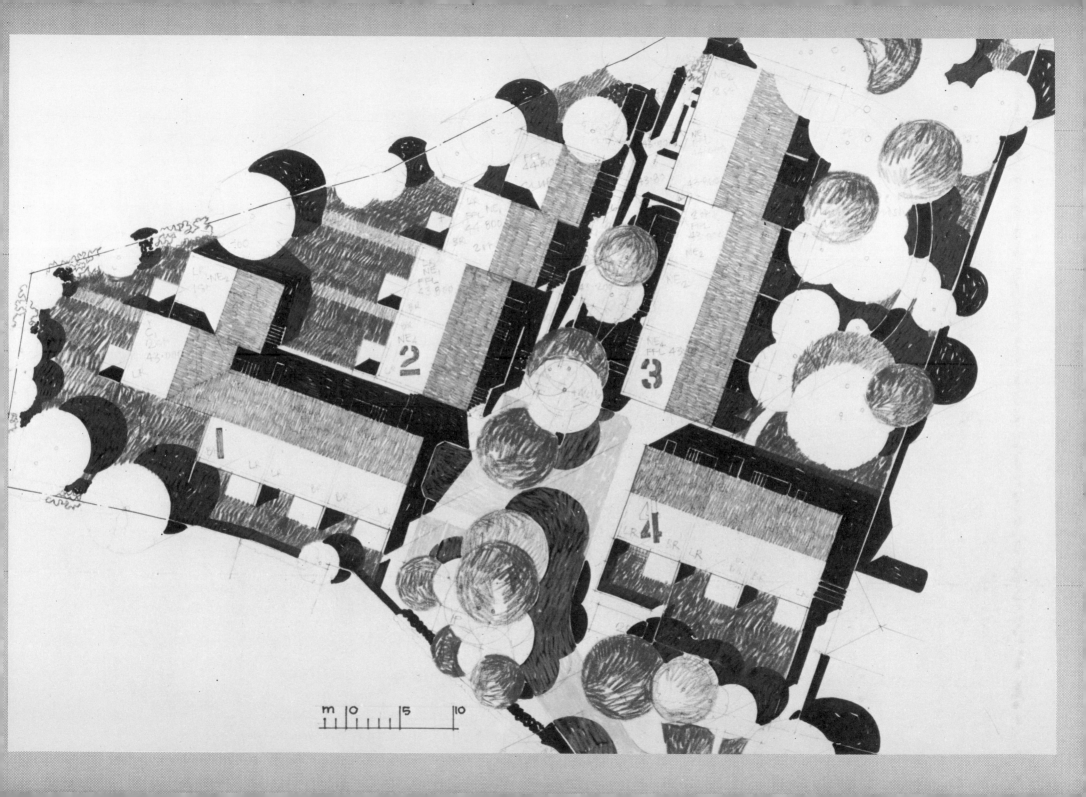

Layout practice

Thornton Road

This site of 0.6 ha is located on an existing GLC estate, and is surrounded by roads on three sides. The layout is based on a density of 181 ppha. A total of 16 car parking spaces has been provided. Vehicular access is from the north and penetrates the site centrally. Car parking areas are grouped along the central access road and extend beyond the service points near block 3.

The development consists of two-storey dwellings, comprising 62 two person old people's flats. A tightly-knit layout has been achieved with the use of controlled-aspect flats (PDP 2210) and 90° corner flats (PDP 2208, 2209, 2224). The layout of the blocks emphasises the direction of the main pedestrian routes, which are orientated towards the shops to the north-east of the site. Some of the terraces (blocks 1, 3, 4) with living rooms and bedrooms turning away from each other, form narrow alleyways giving an intimate scale to the entrances along the route, which are overlooked by kitchen windows.

Two single-store boiler rooms contain gas-fired district heating for the whole development.

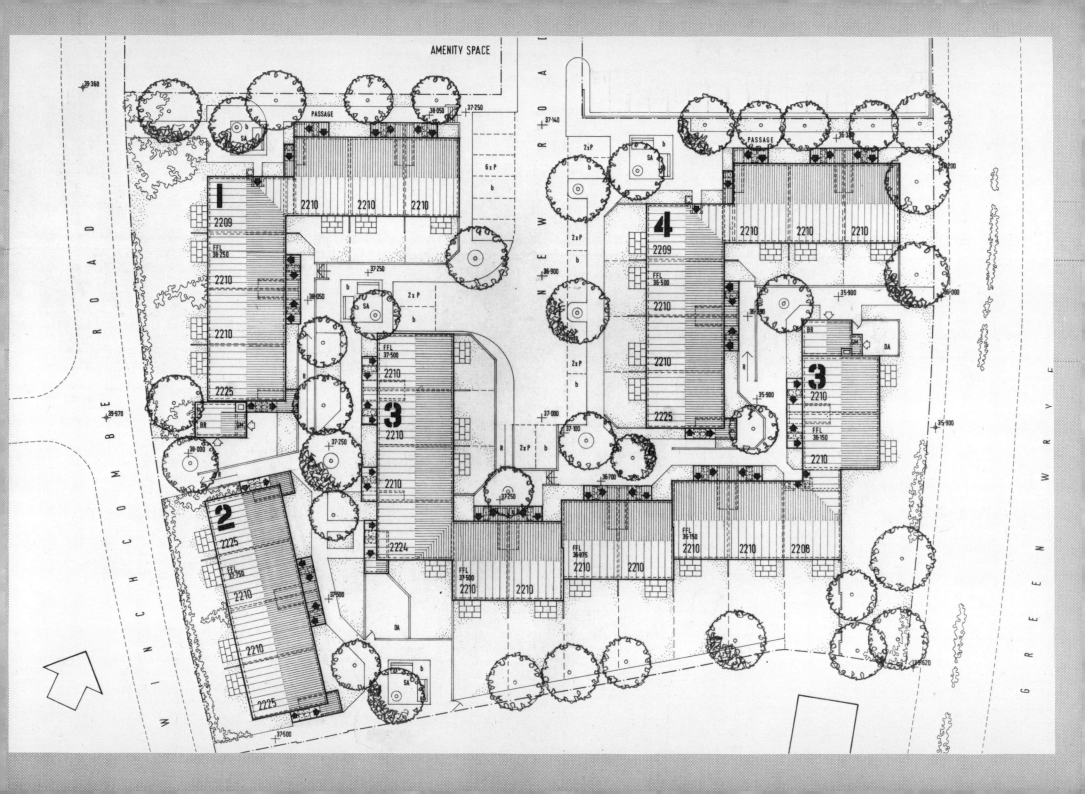

Layout practice

Bryant Avenue

This site totals an area of 0.81 ha. The site is bounded by industrial development to the west, by a heavily used road to the north, by existing residential development to the east and by open land zoned for future hospital development to the south. There is a flood-balancing lake south-west of the site. Landscaped mounding on the northern boundary will protect the site from traffic noise, while an amenity open space to the west will separate the housing from the adjacent industrial development.

The scheme incorporates 256 dwellings at a density of 131 ppha. The dwellings form a series of clusters planned around culs-de-sac, which branch off an access road running diagonally across the site from north-east to south-west. The winding route should inhibit through traffic. There is parking provision for 288 cars.

The scheme is predominantly two-storey and comprises 66 per cent five and six person houses and 34 per cent two person flats. A small number of three-storey flats have been introduced at strategic points to maintain the density and to give added emphasis to the enclosed spaces. The culs-de-sac accommodate car parking areas and service points, and are largely bordered by clusters of dual-aspect north and south entry houses. (PDP 5155, 5162). In many cases the houses are staggered, to produce a greater sense of enclosure. The character of the external spaces is further defined by the careful positioning of controlled-aspect houses (PDP 6101) and corner flats (PDP 2224, 2209).

The houses have related privacy zones within the culs-de-sac which in turn are linked to the car parking spaces. The culs-de-sac are landscaped to form small-scale pedestrian areas which are connected from cluster to cluster in the direction of the main pedestrian route, diagonal to the main access road. All houses are provided with private gardens with separate access on to secondary pedestrian routes.

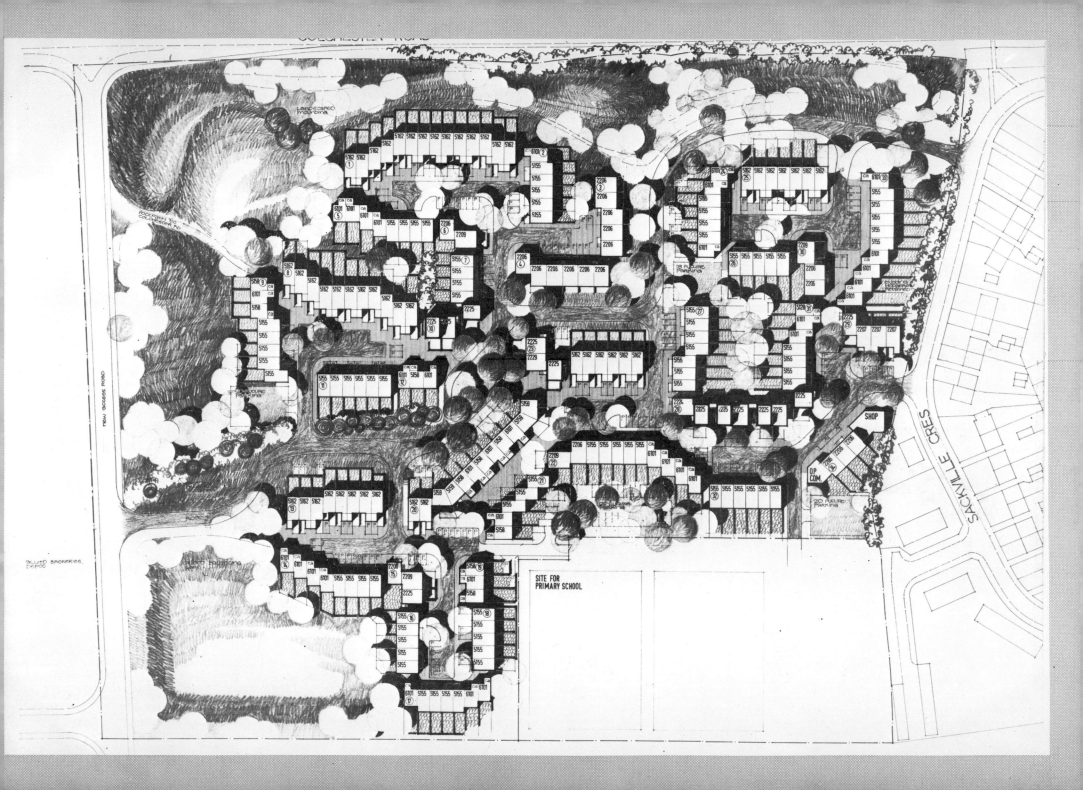

Layout practice
Friern Barnet

General layout

This is a 9.08 ha site which slopes southwards towards the North Circular Road. The layout is planned at a density of 199 ppha and consists of 464 dwellings. The dwelling mix comprises 65.5 per cent family houses with gardens, 31.5 per cent two person flats and 3 per cent bungalows. The flats are arranged in a terrace formation of three-storey blocks. All the houses are two-storeys high. Car parking is ultimately provided for 447 cars.

The houses are arranged in a series of clusters, which are served by four spur roads running at right angles down the site from a distributor road on the northern boundary. The clusters are tightly planned and are interspersed with 'wedges' of existing trees and mature hedges which divide the site into distinctive groupings of dwellings. The single-storey dwellings which adjoin the gable ends of the two-storey houses at the access point to each cluster form a small-scale 'gatehouse' entrance. The three-storey flats form a sequence of crescents along the south side of the distributor road.

Car parking spaces have been provided in close proximity to the houses and generally have been broken into small groups within each housing cluster. The impact of the car will be reduced by the raised planters which have been positioned between the parking areas and the front doors of dwellings. Overflow parking outside the clusters will accommodate extra cars.

Cluster

The detailed layout shows a typical cluster arrangement for 71 dwellings, split into four separate pedestrian/vehicular courts. The two larger courts are almost totally surrounded by dwellings, whereas the remaining clusters have enclosed gardens on their northern sides. The apparent scale of the garden fences or walls is reduced by the positioning of raised planters.

The large clusters are flanked at the entrance point by two projecting bungalows for old people. The northern sides of the clusters are formed by five person dual-aspect south-entry houses (PDP 5162). The eastern side of one cluster and the western side of the other consists of five person dual-aspect houses (PDP 5155). The corners of each cluster are formed by four person single-aspect dwellings (PDP 4204). The southern sides are bordered by five person north-entry houses (PDP 5155). The two smaller clusters are similar but do not include any south-entry houses or single-storey dwellings. Some car parking is provided inside the landscaped courtyards, and further parking spaces form linking elements between the clusters.

The shapes of the gardens have been designed to create a varied interplay between private areas and the communal spaces beyond.

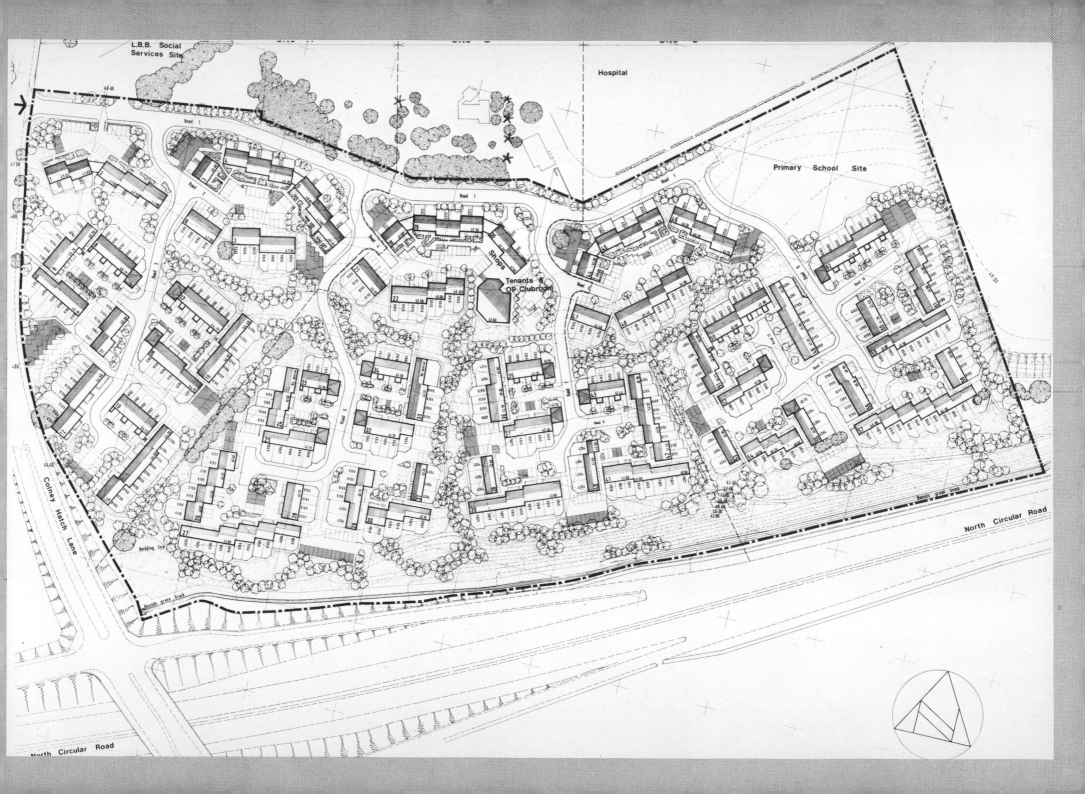

L.B.B. Social
Services Site

Hospital

Primary School Site

Road 1

Shops

Tenants &
OP Clubroom

Colney Hatch Lane

Building line

Bounds Green Brook

North Circular Road

North Circular Road

N

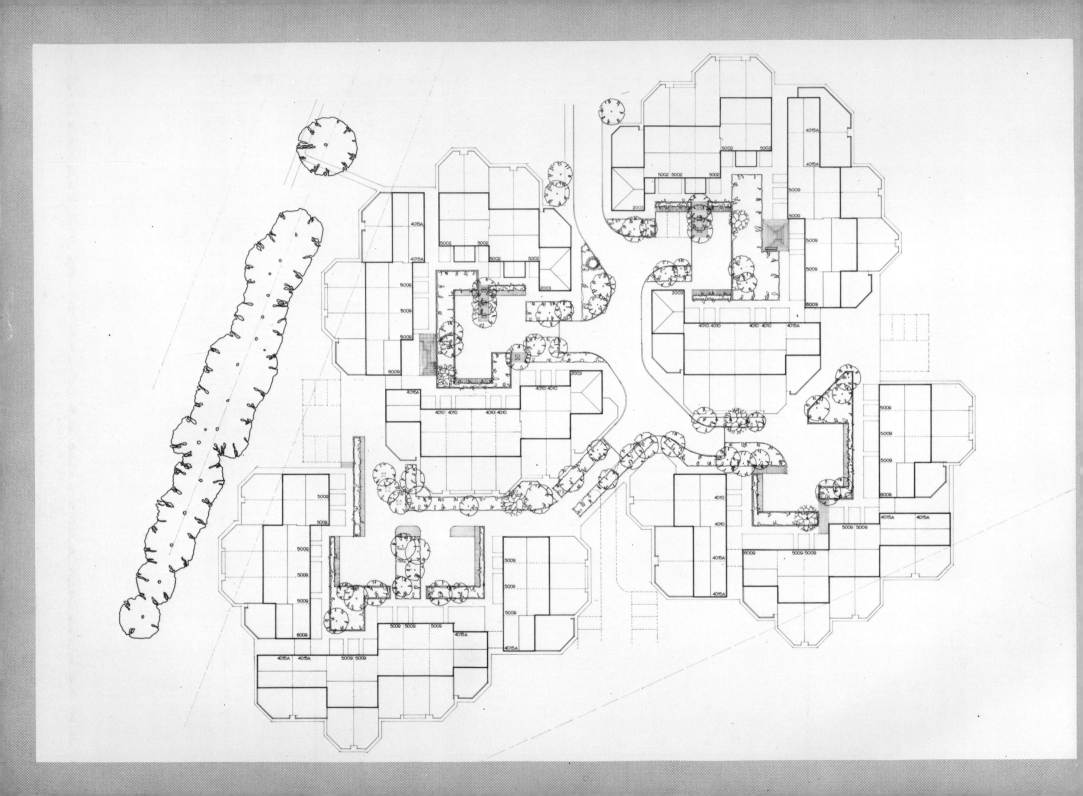

Conclusion

The first aim of any design must be to make proposals appropriate to the specific needs of each individual brief and site. PDPs will be used only on sites which are considered suitable.

It should be stressed that the PDP concept is not seen as a definitive solution to any aspect of the problems of house building, not even to the design problems. PDPs should provide a discipline which will be flexible enough to respond to changes in the prevailing situation and to allow for development in a thoroughly pragmatic way. The range will continue to develop as particular sites and jobs demand. Its advantages can be summed up as follows :

for the designer
*flexibility in layouts
*reduction in the time spent on house design and a
  resultant benefit to the design of the layout
*suitability to different contract methods
*suitability for use in association with the *GLC Good
  Practice Details* for external envelopes

for the building industry
*increased predictability of design and details
*increased standardisation of documentation
*designs which take into account the practices of the
  building industry
*reduction of costs

Credits

Second Edition produced in the
Department of Architecture and Civic Design,
Greater London Council

Architect to the Council   F. B. Pooley, CBE
Housing Architect   Gordon Wigglesworth
Technical Policy Architect   Malcolme Gordon

Graphics and Book Design   John Beake
Editorial Control   David Atwell